A Crown for Staffordshire

Royal Pretenders
in the 14th-16th centuries

Dianne Mannering

For my grandsons, Bruce and Rhett Winwood

Acknowledgments

I would like to thank the many people who have given me so much help and encouragement.

Firstly, Dr Roger Joy who trawled through the chapters during the early stages offering useful advice and suggestions; his help with research was much appreciated as well as his offer to take photographs which involved him in a lot of toing and froing.

To Sylvia M. Everitt MBE for allowing the use of the 16th century panel from the Staffordshire Millennium Embroideries and her as yet incomplete Embroideries of Henry VIII and his wives.

I am delighted too, that Dr Joy has given me permission to use the replicas of Mary Queen of Scots embroideries worked by Sylvia M. Everitt. These will eventually be exhibited in Tutbury Castle.

Walsall Writers' Folio Group – even the members who have little interest in history read various chapters of my manuscript and offered feed-back.

Alan Frost, a friendly genealogist whom I found on the net.

Fellow writers Margaret Dallow and Anne Wilkins for urging me on when I stalled.

The Friends of Dudley Castle

Many thanks to my husband Richard Stevens who shouldered the burden of editing.

Lastly I want to thank Beth Helyer and Adrian Lewis from Coverack Bridges in Cornwall - they have made me a welcome guest in their lovely old Mill House throughout the last two summers and supplied me with a comfortable room in which to write.

Oh, yes…. and my daughter Laura - because she says she was gutted that I didn't give her a mention in my first book.

Dianne Mannering's first book, in full colour, is still available at £9.95:

Staffordshire Millennium Embroideries:
A thousand years of Staffordshire history interpreted through Sylvia M. Everitt's eleven beautiful embroideries.

CHURNET VALLEY BOOKS
1 King Street, Leek, Staffordshire. ST13 5NW 01538 399033
www.leekbooks.co.uk
© Dianne Mannering and Churnet Valley Books 2004
ISBN 1 904546 12 9

Printed and bound by Bath Press

Contents

Bibliography

The Castles & Moated Mansions of Staffordshire & the West Midlands County   Mike Salter
History of the Castle, Priory and Town of Tutbury   Oswald Mosley
Thomas of Lancaster   J R Maddicott
John of Gaunt   S Armitage-Smith
Tutbury Castle   Robert Somerville
The Usurper King   Marie L Bruce
The Princes in The Tower   Alison Weir
The Staffords, Earls of Stafford and Dukes of Buckingham, 1394-1521   Carole Rawcliffe
John Dudley, Duke of Northumberland   David Loades
Britain's Royal Families   Alison Weir
Lady Jane Grey and the House of Suffolk   Alison Plowden
The Mid-Tudor Crisis 1545-1565   David Loades
The Chronicle of Queen Jane   ed. John G Nichols
Sweet Robin   Derek Wilson
On the Trail of Mary Queen of Scots   J Keith Cheetham

Various Ramparts Magazines, the magazine of the Friends of Dudley Castle

OUR THREE FAMOUS CASTLES

Tutbury Castle - Part 1

Tutbury Castle, commanding magnificent views over the valley of the River Dove, was commenced in the early Norman period and has witnessed almost a thousand years of history. A pantheon of monarchs, including Henry IV, James I and Charles I, have passed through its gates and the brilliant John of Gaunt visited the Castle regularly. It served as a prison on three occasions for the romantic Mary Queen of Scots and was besieged by parliamentary forces during the Civil War.

This historic location is the setting for a wide variety of events throughout the year from Viking Spectaculars to formal lectures by leading historians. Opportunities to meet Queen Elizabeth I and Mary Queen of Scots in full costume are available regularly and Tudor tours, specialist lectures and Christmas celebrations feature in the year's programme.

The Castle is licensed for weddings and has high class marquee accommodation for receptions, corporate hospitality functions and private parties.

Tutbury Castle has been chosen by Dr. Roger Joy as the home for the seven Mary Queen of Scots replica embroideries which are currently being crafted by Sylvia M. Everitt MBE. It is expected that these unique embroideries will be on permanent exhibition within the castle from some time in the 2005 season.

For further information please call 01283 812129
Website: www.tutburycastle.com e-mail: infor@tutburycastle.com

The remains of Tutbury Castle. *Courtesy of Dr Roger Joy.*

Stafford Castle - Part 2

Stafford Castle is probably the most viewed castle in Britain for it lies just off the M1 to the east, between Junctions 13 & 14. Much of the original earthworks, built soon after the Norman invasion survive, which makes the castle very special and unique.

During the Civil War in 1643 the castle was held by the Royalists but after a brief skirmish the Parliamentarians won the day. It fell into disrepair until 1813 when Edward Jerningham started to rebuild it, but the work was only partly finished.

In the 20th century the Castle gradually fell into decline again but remained occupied until 1950. In 1961 Lord Stafford gave the castle to Stafford Borough Council. In the 1970s the outstanding importance of the castle was recognised both locally and nationally and a period of conservation and research began.

The Friends of Stafford Castle were formed in the early 1980s to help and support the work of Stafford Borough Council in restoring and promoting Stafford Castle. Over the last 20 years the Friends have fufilled many roles, including providing guides and helping with the digs that have taken place. Further achievements are the creation of two Medieval Herb Gardens and a Visitor Centre at the castle. If you are interested in becoming a Friend please contact our membership secretary:

Derek Warbrick tel: 01785 780592
Email: DerekWarbrick@aol.com

Stafford Castle now   *Courtesy of Dr Roger Joy.*

Dudley Castle - Part 3

Dudley Castle, built first in the early Norman times, has survived many eras and transformations and now looks back on an illustrious history.

To support its venerable history and traditions in an age of speed and wide interests, The Friends of Dudley Castle seeks to promote activities of educational and entertainment interest. We hold meetings, outings, visits, holidays and produce a regular magazine as well as arranging re-enactments, guided tours, outside lectures and costume functions.

If this is your scene, then join us by contacting our Membership Secretary:

Doug Davies
12 Duncroft Walk
Woodsetton
Dudley DY1 4LX
Tel: 01902 678179

The remains of the magnificent Tudor mansion built by John Dudley at Dudley Castle.
Courtesy of John Griffin, Friends of Dudley Castle.

Foreword

Those of us who have read Dianne's book commentating on Sylvia Everitt's Millennium Embroideries will have appreciated her eye for detail and her love for Staffordshire and its history. In this book she gives us a fascinating insight into the complicated struggles of the Middle Ages which touched three Castles in the County and the noble, or sometimes ignoble, families to whom they belonged.

Tutbury, Stafford and Dudley Castles were originally built by their Norman owners, on the instruction of King William, so that they could exercise power over their territories and be seen to do so. Occasionally circumstances or relationships encouraged these people to aspire to greater power, the Throne of England, succession to which was not always too clear. Sometimes they were successful. Sometimes treacherous, sometimes unscrupulous and sometimes rather stupid but their escapades make great stories in the hands of the able raconteur that Dianne is.

We probably all think that we know a bit about these events from our history books, TV programmes or historical novels. Now we are told what really happened in exquisite detail, with fascinating titbits of gossip and interesting family trees.

Child marriages attempting to ensure dynastic succession, teenage young men leading armies because of their seniority of rank, countries laid waste by marauding unpaid troops, executions and worse to remove rivals from the scene, changes in religious allegiance to suit the moment, were all part of those tumultuous years. What is new about political spin?

That Mary Queen of Scots, who had also been Queen of France and declared Queen of England, should be imprisoned in Tutbury Castle by her cousin is an amazing story. It showed how one needed to be in the right place at the right time. Little wonder that her son James, when he became King of the United Kingdom of England, Wales and Scotland, and his son Charles, only to lose his head, believed in the Divine Right of Kings.

Dianne has written a fascinating book which I am sure will be much enjoyed by readers in Staffordshire and beyond.

James Hawley
H.M. Lord-Lieutenant of Staffordshire
Milford September 2004

The Bayeux Tapestry

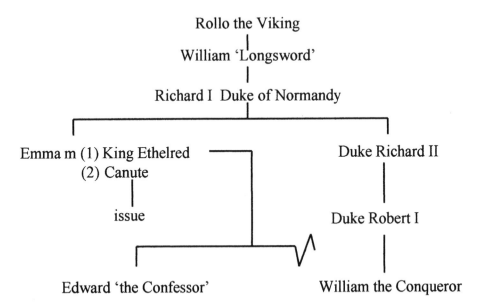

King Ethelred introduced the Normans into the English royal family.
His Norman wife Emma was the great aunt of William the Conqueror.
William and Edward the Confessor were first cousins once removed.

For those of you who like to know who was related to whom and how, I have sought the help of
genealogist Alan Frost. Alan has been delving amongst his ancestors for more than twenty years,
so if your name's Kempshall/Kempsell or Wassell/Wassall do visit his web site at
http://freespace.virgin.net/a.frost

INTRODUCTION

......So You Can Blame Ethelred

According to my computer it is 136 miles from Stafford, the County town of Staffordshire, to the City of London, in Norman and medieval times a journey of something like fourteen days along treacherous lanes and rutted tracks. Good enough reason, you may think, for the castle-owning magnates of Middle England to live their lives away from the political wranglings of King and Court.

It was not that simple. A castle dwelling feudal lord owed allegiance to the Crown. After all, the estates, wealth and status that accompanied his castle were down to the good will of the king. Whether he had been granted his land for services rendered, or inherited it from a politically wily ancestor, the fact remained that these men 'owed' the king. There was no chance of living a life of rustic peace for the castle-owning fraternity; they were the king's right hand men, expected to fight for him, be on hand to advise, make merry with, and above all, be utterly loyal to him.

In theory, the King should have enjoyed the total allegiance of a grateful brotherhood of noblemen, with never a worry about them plotting to steal his crown - and there would have been no book for me to write about the Staffordshire barons and their acquisitive inclinations.

Before I go any further, let me set the scene. There were very few privately owned castles in England prior to the Norman Conquest of 1066 - the concept of a fortress-cum-residence belonging to a mighty overlord was not English. Until William arrived, the Saxon peasants had lived a more or less harmonious existence with their thanes, paying rent, either with money, produce or work. I don't say these serfs and ceorls had an idyllic existence; they were mostly very poor with no chance of improvement. At least, though, before the Conquest, there was no great castle atop the highest hill to remind them that they were a conquered nation.

The idea of peace and harmony is of course in itself an oversimplification because the Vikings had been marauding England for nearly three hundred years. The situation became so fraught that King Ethelred, 'the Unrede', married the daughter of Richard, Duke of Normandy, in an attempt to find an ally against these unwelcome visitors. The Duke of Normandy was the grandson of Rollo, the founder of Normandy and a Viking. Around 915 Rollo had settled with his Scandinavian pillagers in northern France where they went on to build castles, adopt the French language, become Christians and gather a little culture about themselves.

Ethelred died in April 1016 and within the year Canute the Dane was king. He had convinced the English that resistance against his enormous Danish army was futile - and as a belt-and-braces exercise, he married Ethelred's widow Emma in July 1017. Ten years later, Emma became great aunt to the illegitimate baby son of Robert, Duke of Normandy. The baby was William and thirty-nine years later he invaded England on the basis that he had been promised the throne by his uncle, King Edward (the Confessor).

A coin of Edward the Confessor, the dove and the sword
indicating the narrow path he trod to rule England.

Ethelred enjoying his court. He has been vilified by history as 'evil-counselled and feeble'.

So who was Edward the Confessor? Well, he was Ethelred and Emma's son and he followed Canute as King. So you can blame Ethelred for the Conquest because he brought the Normans into the English royal family in the first place.

The new king, William the Conqueror (William I), confiscated the land from the Saxon noble families and doled it out at peppercorn rents to the relatives and supporters who had crossed the channel with him. These favoured few likewise carved up their massive land holdings and leased out estates to their friends and relations, providing themselves with significant incomes.

Throughout the hierarchical layers of this feudal system, each noble had an obligation to his overlord to supply fighting men when required. In return for this promise of militia, the overlord agreed to protect his tenant and his lands when necessary. Thus, once William had established himself as King of England, he also had access to military strength to keep its conquered people subdued.

To make certain that his subjects were in no doubt about the new regime, and who was boss, William instructed his barons to build castles on their recently acquired estates. These first castles served a dual purpose. They were huge wooden buildings, perfect for inspiring awe in the Saxons, most of whom had never seen such formidable structures before; they also provided a secure home for the Norman emigrants who were greatly outnumbered in their adopted country and surrounded by a disgruntled and subjugated native population.

Our aristocracy developed from these first castle-building Norman barons. The remains of their fortresses, much modified over hundreds of years, are our earliest stately homes. Windsor Castle is a perfect example - William's original building was primarily a stronghold; now it is the Queen's favourite home.

The Conqueror was an astute man, well aware that his castle builders were no more than glorified soldiers of fortune who had fallen upon rich pickings because his unlikely plan had succeeded so spectacularly. He knew he had to keep a firm grip on them, so he made sure that their landholdings were fragmented, no noble having an overly large area of the country. He worked on the basis of divide and rule, so that as long as they could not group together he could keep them under control, and they, in return for their estates and wealth, were to give him their total allegiance.

One of these castle-building barons who crossed the Channel with Duke William was Lord Henry of Ferrers.....

Tutbury Castle in the early 17th century. John of Gaunt's Gate is in the foreground.

Part 1
Tutbury Castle

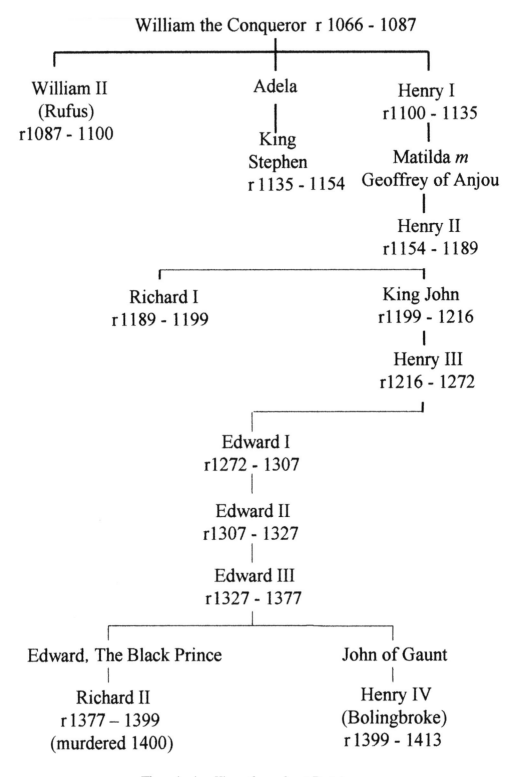

William the Conqueror r 1066 - 1087

William II
(Rufus)
r1087 - 1100

Adela

King
Stephen
r 1135 - 1154

Henry I
r1100 - 1135

Matilda *m*
Geoffrey of Anjou

Henry II
r1154 - 1189

Richard I
r1189 - 1199

King John
r1199 - 1216

Henry III
r1216 - 1272

Edward I
r1272 - 1307

Edward II
r1307 - 1327

Edward III
r1327 - 1377

Edward, The Black Prince

Richard II
r 1377 – 1399
(murdered 1400)

John of Gaunt

Henry IV
(Bolingbroke)
r 1399 - 1413

The reigning Kings throughout Part 1

Chapter 1
A Man With A Vision:
Thomas Plantagenet, Earl of Lancaster

Henry de Ferrers' share of the Conqueror's bonanza was approximately 150 lordships spread throughout Staffordshire, Derbyshire, Leicestershire, Warwickshire and Nottinghamshire. By far his greatest holding was in Derbyshire, but he made his home at Tutbury in the north-east of Staffordshire.

There seems to have been some form of stronghold or defensive earthworks at Tutbury since the 7th century when legend has it that Offa, King of the Mercians, held court there. At the time of the Norman Conquest there was still a ruined, wooden structure on the site.

Henry was granted the Manor of Tutbury in 1071 and immediately commenced to build his castle there as his chief home and the administrative headquarters of his scattered estates. Very pleasant this lofty vantage point must have been too, with the River Dove flowing through his meadows on one side and a huge tract of hunting forest and woodland on the other.

Little more than this is known of the man who established the Ferrers' family fortunes here in England, except that Henry was appointed by King William as one of the commissioners to oversee the compilation of the Domesday Book in 1086.

The Conqueror died not long after the Domesday Book was completed and of course, in the fullness of time, Henry and the rest of the original Norman settlers followed him to the grave. Their descendants became careless of the fact that they owed their castles, their fat livings and their allegiance to their king. These men forgot that the Conqueror had made their forefathers wealthy in exchange for support and loyalty, qualities they failed to demonstrate when the direct Norman line ran into trouble.

The year was 1120 and one of William's sons, King Henry, had been on the throne for twenty years. He was married with two sons and a daughter, Matilda. On the evening of 25th November his two sons boarded the *White Ship* at Barfleur to sail to England, following their father, whose ship had left earlier in the day. There was much drinking and merrymaking aboard the vessel and in an attempt to catch up with their father's ship, the Princes urged the boatmen to row with more speed than care. The boat came to grief on the Raz de Gatteville rocks, with only one survivor, a butcher's boy, who told how the two Princes, having cleared the wreck, returned to save the life of their illegitimate half sister - and perished in the attempt.

Henry was devastated; he was left with only one legitimate offspring, his daughter Matilda. This disaster presented a problem that, for the next 400 years or so, our Staffordshire castle-owning families milked - that there was no written law of succession to the throne of England.

Snippet   Queen Matilda's husband Geoffrey, Count of Anjou and father to King Henry II, gave us the name Plantagenet from the sprig of broom he wore in his hat (latin - planta genista). As a dynastic name it wasn't formally adopted until the 15th century.

The Normans in their homeland embraced the French Salic law which dictated that there were no rights for a female to succeed to the throne. In England, we had no hard and fast rule about the succession. Primogeniture - where the crown passes from father to son and for want of a son to a daughter was not yet law or even an accepted principal. Before the Conquest, the new king was chosen from a list of delegates whose only prerequisite was that they should have at least some vague connection to the royal family. Since William the Conqueror's death we had been ruled by two of his sons, William 'Rufus' who died unmarried, and then Henry. As Henry had two legitimate sons, it had never been necessary for him to consider the succession - until the White Ship disaster.

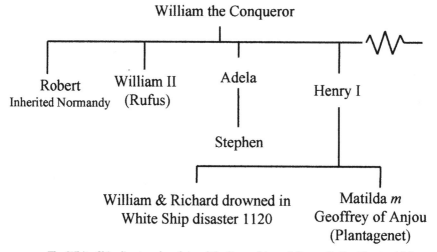

The White Ship disaster also claimed the lives of two of Henry I's illegitimate children.

Henry arranged a marriage between his daughter Matilda and thirteen year old Geoffrey of Anjou (later called Plantagenet) and made his nobles, mostly descendants of William's Norman settlers, promise to allow the crown to pass to this pair when he died.

But, as we have already seen, this generation of noblemen had forgotten their loyalties and did not keep their promises to the King. When Henry died in 1135, they decided that a woman was not fit to rule and voted the crown to Matilda's cousin, Stephen.

The result was 19 years of civil war while Stephen and Matilda fought over the throne. As the nobles had a feudal obligation to supply the ruler with fighting men in accordance with their landed wealth, there could be no sitting on the fence; sides had to be taken. Henry de Ferrers' son, Robert, who was now the Lord of Tutbury Castle, chose to back Stephen and for his loyalty (or disloyalty to Henry?), the new King created him Earl of Derby in 1138.

So already, only 70 years after the Conqueror had instructed his nobles to build fortifications so that they could protect his interests, the descendants of his fortune hunting barons had chosen not to obey King Henry's carefully planned instructions and instead, had used their castles to back up a treacherous betrayal.

A couple of generations later, Earl Robert's grandson, William de Ferrers, again seems to have forgotten where his loyalties were due and joined two of Henry II's sons, Richard and Geoffrey in an unsuccessful revolt against their father. As a punishment for this treachery, Earl William's castle was demolished. The friendship between the Earl and Prince Richard continued, and years later, when Richard was King Richard I (the Lionheart), William accompanied him to the Holy Land and died there at the siege of Acre.

The castle was rebuilt before the end of the 12th century, and in stone, so this time Tutbury was an immensely strong fortification. The castle's new owner, Earl William's son, also William, was a steadfast friend of King John who visited Tutbury on several occasions during his troubled reign. William was with John when he lost his jewels in the Wash; he was a signatory to his will, and he was at his bedside when he died; a true and loyal liegeman.

The 5th Earl of Derby was yet another William and along with his castle, he inherited from his father a propensity to gout. The debility was so acute that even as a young man he had to be carried about in a horse-litter, and he died after being accidentally toppled from his carriage. His fortune fell to his infant son, Robert.

Young Earl Robert enjoyed a strong relationship with the mature Henry III and dusty legend tells that Queen Eleanor stayed at Tutbury Castle while her husband mounted an expedition against the Welsh. Later though, in 1264, Robert joined Simon de Montfort, Earl of Leicester, in an armed rebellion and was involved in capturing the King and his heir, Prince Edward. The Prince escaped and retaliated with an awesome attack on Tutbury, murdering villagers, laying waste the surrounding countryside and destroying the castle. Robert was taken prisoner, but King Henry pardoned him and gave him his freedom.

Incredibly, the Earl seemed determined to dismantle everything that his forebears had spent their lives consolidating, and within a year of the King's pardon he was involved in another revolt. Irresolute as King Henry often was, forgiveness was not an option after this second treachery and Robert was stripped of his heritage.

Just at the time of Robert's downfall another of Henry's sons, Prince Edmund (Crouchback), was in need of the wealth and trappings befitting a prince of royal blood. Plundering the King's estates to provide for his son was not the best option because this diluted the royal wealth and power, so a few dissident noblemen came in very handy at such times because their confiscated estates made extremely useful handouts. And so it was that

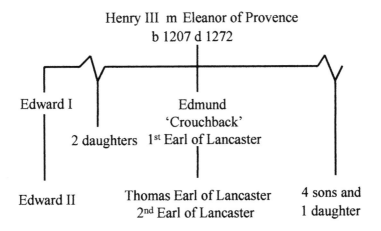

Edward I was Thomas of Lancaster's uncle.

the 22 year old Crouchback was granted the lands and titles of the rebel barons Robert Ferrers and Simon de Montfort with, a little while later, the honour of Lancaster added to the package. This vast territorial bounty was all streamlined into an Earldom and Edmund became the 1st Earl of Lancaster. King Henry's gift to his son was the first link in the chain of events that eventually brought Tutbury Castle into the ownership of the future kings and queens of England, the current owner being Her Majesty, Queen Elizabeth II.

It would be fair to mention here that there is a lot of ancient text stored in dusty archives which claims that Robert was unfairly ousted from his dynastic inheritance, the unhappy victim of legal chicanery. However, when you get down to the nitty-gritty, Robert must have known the score for disloyalty to his King. He was disloyal and he lost his lands.... is there any more to be said? I doubt that William the Conqueror would have thought so.

The first Earl of Lancaster seems not to have been overly impressed with the ruined Tutbury Castle and it remained neglected and unused during his lifetime. This, of course, was no help to the villagers who had suffered at the hands of Prince Edward's army during Earl Ferrer's rebellions. For the greater part of the previous two centuries the villagers' livelihoods had been enhanced and shaped by the affluence flowing from the busy comings and goings at the castle - a case of 'the gravy trickling down'. Now, with the castle forsaken, there was no opportunity for the local population to get back on their feet.

Crouchback died in 1296 and the Lancastrian estates were inherited by his elder son Thomas, 2nd Earl of Lancaster. Henry III was long gone by this time and the young Prince Edward who had devastated Robert Ferrer's estates now reigned as Edward I. He was, of course, Thomas's uncle.

Thomas repaired Tutbury Castle and used it as his principal residence, living and entertaining there in splendid extravagance. Once again the village and the surrounding locality enjoyed a prosperity which flowed off the back of the lord's residence. Thomas, though, was not a happy man. He had been married at fifteen (presumably without much say in the matter) to Alice de Lacy, daughter of the Earl of Lincoln. This marriage was decidedly unsuccessful for both parties. There were no children and seemingly, no companionship.

Sir Oswald Mosley, in his 1832 *History of the Castle, Priory and Town of Tutbury,* accuses Thomas of being *'reserved and neglectful'* whilst Alice he says was *'giddy and thoughtless'*. There is scant evidence of their personal relationship, but in the light of the very public breakdown of their marriage, perhaps these cameos are reasonably accurate. Alice ran away to live with a lover whose circumstances were modest compared to what she had been used to all of her life. She did this knowing that she would forfeit her father's estates that had been absorbed into the Earldom of Lancaster.

As for Thomas, amongst his surviving letters there are few which give an insight into the man behind the earldom, though reports of dealings with his tenants seem harsh and unforgiving, even by medieval standards. He grew up with great expectations because his uncle, Edward I, and Queen Eleanor, were troubled by a lack of male heirs. When Thomas was born in 1278 the King's first two sons had already died and there was just one male heir, five years old Alfonso. The Queen had five more daughters before her fourteenth child, Edward, was born. Within four months of Edward's arrival, Alfonso died, so there was still only one male heir and although there were more babies, none were sons.

There were, of course, the daughters, but we still had no written law of succession, so their position was not clear. As the Royal family and barons were mostly French speaking descendants of the Normans there was every reason for Thomas to suspect that if the crown came up for grabs, the nobles would look to their roots and favour the French Salic law. This would mean a repeat performance of the Matilda and Stephen debacle when the direct female heir was put aside for the nearest male heir.

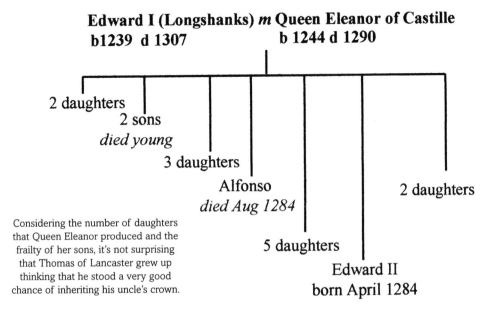

Edward I (Longshanks) *m* **Queen Eleanor of Castille**
b1239 d 1307   **b 1244 d 1290**

2 daughters

2 sons
died young

3 daughters

Alfonso
died Aug 1284

2 daughters

5 daughters

Edward II
born April 1284

Considering the number of daughters that Queen Eleanor produced and the frailty of her sons, it's not surprising that Thomas of Lancaster grew up thinking that he stood a very good chance of inheriting his uncle's crown.

Thomas's father was the next in line to the throne behind the King's son Edward, and behind him was Thomas. So, when Crouchback died, Thomas became heir presumptive. He grew up knowing that it only needed his cousin Edward to follow his three brothers to an early grave and he would inherit the throne. Growing up in such uncertain times with a crown dangling tantalisingly close was surely enough to warp anyone's personality.

He lived through his teenage years with these illustrious hopes, but at the age of 21, Thomas saw the crown drifting away. Prince Edward, five years his junior, was maturing into a strapping youth who did not look like following his brothers to an early grave. Worse still, the sixty year old King, who had been a widower for nine years, married the King of France's eighteen year old sister. Within three years they had produced two healthy sons and, to add insult to injury, the eldest was named Thomas. The old King provided his young wife with a daughter to go with her two sons and then died, leaving Thomas's cousin as Edward II.

But while Thomas had slipped smoothly into his titles and estates when his father died, his cousin enjoyed no such easy transition into his kingdom. Firstly, when his father, Edward I (the Hammer of the Scots) died in July 1307 still hammering the Scots, he bequeathed to his heir £60,000 of treasury debts, unpaid soldiers and an ongoing war with the new King of Scotland, Robert the Bruce.

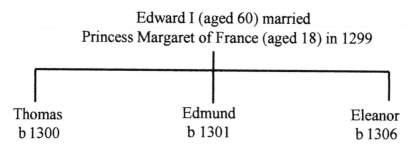

Edward I (aged 60) married
Princess Margaret of France (aged 18) in 1299

Thomas	Edmund	Eleanor
b 1300	b 1301	b 1306

Edward I died in 1307: He fathered nineteen children between his two wives.

Secondly, shortly before his death, the old King had found out that his son's friendship with a young Gascon nobleman, Piers Gaveston, did not stop at the bedroom door. There was unpleasantness between father and son over this relationship and the courtier was packed off home to Gascony.

Gaveston was hardly off the shores of Dover when the King died. Edward II, without even waiting for his father's funeral, recalled his friend to England. Before the year was out, the new King had endowed Gaveston with two hugely inappropriate gifts. In August he made him Earl of Cornwall and a few months later, he was given a royal bride. The earldom brought the young man a vast territorial endowment and the bride was Edward's niece, Margaret de Clare, daughter of his sister, the Countess of Gloucester.

The barons met Edward's acts of munificence towards his favourite with hostile disdain. The earldom of Cornwall was possibly the greatest gift at the King's disposal and a royal bride was tremendously sought after. The lords were of the opinion that the earldom should more rightly have been bestowed upon one of the King's young half brothers. As for little Margaret de Clare, it is very likely that several of the nobles had earmarked her from the day she was born as a potential daughter-in-law.

Worse was in store. Many worthy noblemen with years of political experience were dismissed and the besotted Edward installed replacement officials chosen, more or less, at Gaveston's whim.

An even greater insult was in store for the lords. Early the following year the King left for France to marry the French King's daughter Isabella and, ignoring his elder statesmen, he appointed Gaveston as his Regent.

Snippet When Edward I married the King of France's sister Margaret in 1299, he also arranged the betrothal of his heir Prince Edward to the French King's daughter Princess Isabella, aged about five years.

The lords were in outrage. Ever since the Conquest, the king's chief nobles had enjoyed the right to help him rule the country - it went with their titles and their castles. Edward I, who was a man with plenty of political foresight and ability, had leaned heavily on sage councillors such as Thomas's father-in-law, the Earl of Lincoln. The new King sought only to listen to the advice of his young friend.

Thomas in particular nursed a rabid antagonism towards Gaveston, as well as his cousin the King. In the years when there had been a very real possibility that the crown might settle on his own head he had perhaps nurtured dreams about how he would rule the country. Now, the political shambles brought about by his cousin's reliance on this inept

A representation of Edward II and Gaveston as lovers.

favourite served only to make him determined that Edward should be forced to rule the kingdom effectively.

A reform committee was established and, calling themselves the Lords Ordainers, they set out to shackle the King and disempower Gaveston. Thomas's father-in-law, the Earl of Lincoln - dubbed 'Burst Belly' by Gaveston - was one of the chief Ordainers. Though the Earl of Lincoln was no great fan of Edward, he was far more interested in good government than promoting his son-in-law's personal vendetta against the King, and while he lived, he curbed Thomas's worst excesses.

But the Earl died soon after the Lords Ordainers were formed and Thomas, in right of his wife, inherited the earldoms of Lincoln and Salisbury. These two, added to the three he already possessed, Lancaster, Leicester and Derby, made him by far the wealthiest noble in the country. Such affluence and status, coupled with his animosity towards Edward and Gaveston, automatically propelled Thomas into the forefront of the opposition party, but with an axe to grind as much as a sincere wish for political stability.

The aggrieved lords, armed with their list of reforms, insisted that the King should strip Gaveston of his titles and exile him. It was alleged that the young man was in breach of the Ordinances (laws) in that he had encouraged the King to act in ways contrary to the good of the realm. Reluctantly, Edward sent his favourite away, but within weeks the young Gascon was back in England and he spent Christmas at Windsor with the King.

Thomas's party, exasperated and frustrated, were no longer in a mood for negotiation with Edward. They prepared for civil war and when the King became aware of their intentions, he and Gaveston took flight, trailing Edward's reluctant young wife, Queen Isabella along with them. For some reason the King thought that Robert the Bruce would give Gaveston protection in Scotland and so they trekked north. At Newcastle-on-Tyne news reached them that the Scots' king was not prepared to guarantee Gaveston's well being and the fugitives found themselves stranded with Thomas's army hot on their heels.

By the time Thomas arrived in Newcastle, his quarry was gone. He found a seething and humiliated Queen Isabella, pregnant with her first child, who had been dumped along with the baggage train. The King and his companion made their escape to Tynemouth and from there by boat to Scarborough. Thomas was as closely related to Queen Isabella as he was to Edward. His mother had been married to the King of Navarre before she married Crouchback, and her daughter by him, Joan, had married Philip IV King of France. Isabella was their daughter, so Thomas's mother was Isabella's grandmother.

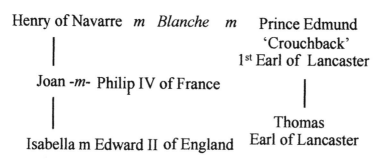

Thomas's mother was Queen Isabella's grandmother

> Snippet For those of you who like to put a handle on a relationship, Thomas was Queen Isabella's 'uncle of the half blood' and she his 'niece of the half blood'.

So Thomas and Isabella shared strong blood ties as well as a common foe in Gaveston. After capturing Isabella (in effect a rescue), the Earl promised that he would not rest until her husband and Gaveston had been separated. He learned that Gaveston was at Scarborough Castle and that Edward had made his way to York to gather an army, so he positioned his forces between Scarborough and York to make sure that the pair could not join up.

Although the King had instructed Gaveston not to leave the safety of the castle, he was persuaded to do so after the Earls of Pembroke and Surrey besieged the stronghold for a couple of weeks. Pembroke, who prided himself on being true to his word, promised the young man that if he surrendered he would be escorted unharmed to London and delivered to Parliament to make a decision about his future. But not everyone who had helped winkle Gaveston out of Scarborough Castle was happy with this chivalry. Many of the nobles felt that parliamentary discussion would lead only to banishment again. They were in no mind for a velvet glove; they wanted the King's favourite eradicated once and for all.

It was early summer and the weather was pleasant when Pembroke and his men started the long journey to London with their prisoner. At Banbury, the Earl arranged a stopover to visit his wife at one of his nearby estates, Brampton. During the night, while Pembroke was away, Guy Beauchamp, the Earl of Warwick, arrived with a party of armed men and broke into Gaveston's lodgings, hauled him from his bed and hustled him away, barefoot and dressed only in his night-shirt. It was the end of Gaveston's leisurely return to London; instead, he was taken to Warwick Castle and flung into the dungeon.

Thomas, Earl of Lancaster, along with Humphrey de Bohun, Earl of Hereford, and Edmund Fitzalan, Earl of Arundel, were not long in turning up at Warwick Castle where Gaveston's fate was now decided without the help of Parliament. When one of the earls suggested that execution was not necessarily the answer, the reply (possibly Thomas's) *'you have caught the fox; if you let him go, you will have to hunt him again'* served to focus everyone's mind and Gaveston's fate was sealed. The young man was found guilty of treason by authority of the Ordinances in that he had misled and ill-advised the King.

Just ten days after he was snatched from the Earl of Pembroke's custody, Gaveston was taken from Warwick Castle, marched a couple of miles on to Lancastrian land at Blacklow Hill and beheaded. Lancaster, Arundel and Hereford skulked at a distance, while Warwick isolated himself from events by staying put in his castle.

Gaveston's head was later presented to Thomas. This, coupled with the execution taking place on a Lancastrian estate, suggests that although Thomas was not present at the abduction, he was the driving force behind the business. King Edward was certainly of this opinion; as far as he was concerned his cousin Thomas was a dead man walking after Gaveston's fate. Edward had the head sewn back into place before the body was embalmed and he swore that his friend would remain unburied until his death had been avenged.

As events turned out this personal quest for retribution had to be put on hold during the latter part of 1313 while England prepared to do battle with Scotland. The King summoned his barons to prepare for war, but Thomas along with the Earls of Warwick, Surrey and Arundel refused to do any more than supply the minimum number of knights and men-at-arms stipulated under their feudal obligations. Thomas, the ringleader again, quoted the Ordinances as the reason for not supporting the King, on the basis that he ought not to have committed his magnates to war without prior discussion.

In fact, extra soldiers at Bannockburn would not have helped the King. Defeat there had nothing to do with a lack of militia and much to do with battle technique. But the lessons of warfare learned during this battle were to stand Edward in good stead when, six years later, one of his commanders came face to face with Thomas of Lancaster.

With the King's ignominious defeat against Robert the Bruce in June 1314, his promised vengeance against Gaveston's murderers became a long-term project. So, later that year he organised a magnificent funeral for his favourite. Thomas and most of the barons, who had so despised the man during his life, stood aloof refusing to attend his grand send-off.

While the King licked his 1314 battle wounds and grieved the loss of his friend, Thomas and his extremists took political control. By way of the Ordinances they pushed

Edward II marries Isabella at Boulogne in France.

The medal struck on the occasion of John, Duke of Lancaster's marriage to Constancia of Castile.

forward their plans to force good government onto King and country. Thomas of Lancaster, cousin to the King, had got this far because of the bed he was born in and the woman he had married. He now had to prove himself worthy of his backers. Unfortunately, once he was poised to carry the lords and the country with him, it became evident that Thomas had little inclination for the 'nuts and bolts' of government. He delegated too much and lacked the qualities of leadership required to hold his supporters together.

King Edward, two-faced, devious and cunning, was able to take advantage of his cousin's weakness by continually causing friction between him and his followers. One such coup involved Thomas's wife, for it was at this time that Alice ran away to live with her lover. This was a humiliating situation for the first earl of the country. The King's part in the elopement seems to have been little more than to encourage one of Thomas's allies, the Earl of Surrey to assist Alice in her plans, and when Thomas learned of Surrey's part in his wife's desertion, he attacked his former friend's estates, and the King, happy to increase discord between the two men, sent an army to assist the beleaguered Surrey.

The upshot of the feud was the formation of the Middle Party, consisting of lords who believed that no effective government could be established while the King and the premier Earl were at loggerheads. At the head of the new party was the Earl of Pembroke whose declared aim was to bring about reconciliation between the King and his cousin. He was, however, no friend of Thomas - he had not been since the June night in 1312 when Gaveston had been abducted from his care.

Surrey welcomed the new party after Thomas's ravaging of his estates and he joined Pembroke's cause. Gradually, Lancaster began to lose other supporters to the more moderate Middle Party. The country struggled along for the next few years with the ranks of the new party gradually swelling. Nobles who did not necessarily agree with Pembroke's moderating ideals supported his party line because they disagreed with Thomas's uncompromising implementation of the Ordinances.

By 1318 Pembroke had persuaded Thomas and the King to put on a show of reconciliation. But nobody was fooled by this public kiss of friendship; Thomas still refused to patch up his quarrel with Surrey, and the King was still harbouring revenge for Gaveston's murder.

It was, in effect Gaveston's successor who finally brought the quarrel between Thomas and his kinsman to a head. The King had attached himself to another favourite, Hugh Despenser, the Younger. He had been at court for many years but now became Edward's constant companion and adviser. To the frustrated lords, Hugh Despenser, and to a lesser extent his father, also Hugh, was a re-enactment of the Gaveston situation. Both men were showered with political appointments, huge financial hand-outs and like Gaveston, Hugh the Younger was given a royal wife.

The two men were rapacious in the extreme and Edward did not have the sense or inclination to curb their acquisitiveness. He allowed them to twist the law so that estates could be confiscated from their rightful owners on some vague pretext of a misdemeanour.

Snippet Here in Staffordshire, John de Sutton the owner of Dudley Castle fell foul of the Despenser's avarice. After Thomas's rebellion they accused him of supporting the Earl. He was imprisoned and lived with the threat of execution until he signed over estates, manors and Dudley Castle to the younger Despenser.

The last straw came when, in 1321, Hugh Despenser the Younger persuaded Edward to confiscate the estates of a Marcher lord (a noble with lands bordering Wales) who had recently died, and whose son-in-law, Sir John Mowbray had taken the inheritance. The Marcher Lords, in particular Henry de Bohun, Earl of Hereford, Roger Mortimer of Wigmore, Roger Mortimer of Chirk, Sir Robert Clifford, Sir Hugh Audley and Sir Roger Damory, became alarmed at Edward's interference with their hereditary customs and immediately took up arms.

It happened that Thomas's younger brother Henry had inherited in right of his wife, lands on the Marches, as Lord of Kidwelly, and so Thomas, ever on the look out for an acrimonious cause against the King, took up the Marchers' crusade.

By supporting the Marchers' quarrel, Thomas found himself a new tranche of allies to help him in his campaign against Edward and the now hated Despensers. After devastating the Despenser estates in Glamorgan, the Marcher Lords advanced on London, while Thomas addressed Parliament, insisting that the Despensers were to be exiled and their lands forfeited. He threatened that if the favourites were not banished the nobles would *utterly renounce their homage and set up a new ruler.*

To renounce their homage - in other words, to refuse to accept the King as their overlord flew in the face of the whole fabric of kingship introduced by William the Conqueror two and a half centuries before. The King saw little room for negotiation. The implication was that Edward's two young sons and his two half brothers would be side-stepped and Lancaster would take the crown. Reluctantly, he allowed the Despensers to be stripped of their estates and they were banished from the Kingdom.

The nobles were exultant at their success and notwithstanding his shaky track record, they again turned to Thomas to continue the impetus and force the King into good and fair policies. As before, Lancaster fell short of proving himself worthy of his followers. Now that the King was deprived of his advisers and in need of strong advice and support, the Earl lacked a concrete plan to push home the political advantage the Marchers had won for him. In opposition Thomas was turbulent and disruptive, but when he had the chance to put his ideals into action, he lost his way.

For the rest of 1321 the King and the Earl jockeyed desperately for position. Thomas still insisted that Edward should rule in accordance with the Ordinances, even though some of these reforms had already proved unworkable and unpopular. Compromise, though, was not in Thomas's book and gradually, the nobles who had backed him began to realign their affinities with the King.

Edward, seeing the tide turn, recalled the Despensers from exile and with their aid, began a determined campaign to rid himself of Thomas and his thinning band of supporters. The Marchers who had armed themselves and advanced on London had, in effect, committed treason and now the King retaliated by attacking their estates. The two Mortimers and Sir Hugh Audley surrendered without a fight, but the Earl of Hereford with Roger Damory and John Mowbray fled north to Thomas, who had mustered his private army at his castle in Pontefract.

Snippet Pontefract Castle had come Thomas's way via his father-in-law Henry de Lacy.

In January 1322 Thomas realised that the King's forces were moving towards Staffordshire with the obvious intention of attacking his midlands estates. With his main seat under threat, he sent one of his most trusted followers, Sir Robert Holland, north to collect reinforcements, and made for Tutbury.

As soon as he arrived at Burton-on-Trent, Thomas took possession of the Burton bridge, which protected his castle, just a few miles to the north-west. His soldiers, ill-disciplined and hungry, were allowed to rampage all over the town demanding food and accommodation and no doubt indulging in a spot of rape and pillage.

There had been snow, a thaw and then torrential rain, so the Trent was in full flood when the King's army arrived in the area. As Thomas's men were in possession of the only bridge, Edward's commanders were left with just two choices. Firstly, they could attack the bridge, which would be difficult because it was very long and very narrow - a medieval bridge was built to accommodate nothing wider than a packhorse train. Alternatively they could make camp and wait for the river to subside.

The decision was made to camp and wait. While they did so, a disgruntled local who had perhaps been forced to feed or accommodate Lancaster's soldiers, came to the camp. He told the King's commander that the river had subsided near a tiny village called Walton-on-Trent, just five miles upstream from Burton.

On March 10th, while Thomas's soldiers were kept busy protecting the Burton bridge against a determined and surprise onslaught, the main body of the royalist army slipped away and crossed the river at Walton.

Thomas abandoned the bridge, set Burton afire to cause confusion and retreated to Tutbury Castle. Now Thomas learned that his ally Holland had defected to the royalists with the much needed reinforcements. Sir Robert Holland had been a butler in Thomas's household and it was through the Earl that he had gained his knighthood. This unexpected defection would have had a staggering effect on morale.

Thomas's supporters now began to examine, with a great deal of unease, the unpleasant consequences of having backed a loser. Thomas decided to make for his stronghold at Pontefract and an immediate evacuation began. This exit from Tutbury Castle was so fraught with haste that Roger Damory and several other wounded allies were left behind to be taken prisoner. Thomas's baggage train, including three chests of silver coin brought in to pay the troops, also seem to have been abandoned or unguarded during the evacuation, because it went missing without trace. King Edward moved into the castle and spent the next few days thoroughly looting the place and sending out proclamations ordering that Lancaster and his rebels should be apprehended as traitors. Rumours about Thomas's three chests of silver abounded and so, before setting off in pursuit of the rebels, Edward set up a commission of enquiry to investigate what had happened to the treasure.

It is generally believed that Thomas was expecting reinforcements from Scotland but none materialised. Whether Robert the Bruce let him down or whether there was never any promise has not been firmly established. The Earl's supporters decided to put distance between themselves and the King - their best chances of survival lay in holing up somewhere as far away from him as possible and waiting for him to calm down. Thomas, relying on his blood ties with Edward to save his neck, wanted to remain at Pontefract.

Thomas's men knew nothing of the ploy until the King's troops fanned out in the snow covered meadows below the castle, and having backed a loser, tempers became frayed - his followers could not rely on close royal kinship to save their lives and Sir Robert Clifford threatened Lancaster with his sword. Thomas agreed to move further north and immediately the rebels set off on the long march to his newly built castle at Dunstanburgh in Northumberland. It is possible that Clifford's insistence on trekking northwards was also because he still held out hopes that Robert the Bruce might be making his way south with reinforcements.

On 16th March the rebels reached Boroughbridge, 30 miles from Pontefract, where they found Andrew Harclay, Earl of Carlisle guarding the bridge across the Ure. There was no going back, but to go forward meant crossing the bridge. Lancaster divided his troops. Hereford, the only high ranking peer still clinging to Thomas's cause, and Clifford set about taking the bridge by direct assault while their leader attempted to cross the river with his cavalry at a nearby ford to attack from behind. Hereford lost his life to a spear thrust up through the bridge planking. Clifford was wounded and taken prisoner. The enemy archers now drove the leaderless and utterly demoralised infantry into retreat.

Down river, the lessons that Harclay had learned from the Scots eight years before at Bannockburn did him stout service. Remembering the 1314 rout, the commander formed his troops into a schiltrom - basically, a large circle of men heaving 15ft pikes. This configuration, continually on the move and looking something like a giant hedgehog, formed an impenetrable and deadly barrier. Lancaster, who had refused to support King Edward on his Scottish campaign, had no experience of the idea and was unable to make inroads against the enemy. When he learned that he had lost his two commanders on the bridge, he sent to Harclay asking for a truce until the following day. The next morning, 17th March, Thomas found that Hereford's and Clifford's leaderless troops had skulked away. All his dreams and plans, his scheming and tyranny had finally come to nothing. He surrendered and was taken back to his castle at Pontefract where the King awaited him.

Revenge is sweet; Edward had waited ten years for this moment. Thomas was tried within the walls of his own castle and the King himself read out the treasonable charges against his cousin. Men who had in years past been Thomas's allies against the King's misrule were there now to sit in judgement against him. Pembroke and Surrey who had besieged Scarborough Castle and persuaded Piers Gaveston to surrender; Arundel who had watched with Thomas from behind a tree while the detested favourite was beheaded; all now had his life in their hands.

It took little time to decide that Lancaster was guilty of treason and he was sentenced to a traitor's death - meaning that he was to be hung, drawn and quartered. His noble birth and Edward's wish only to see him suffer the same as Gaveston - no more - saved Thomas from this fate, and the sentence was reduced to beheading.

Edward was still mindful of Gaveston's final, squalid exit though, and he insisted that Thomas should suffer, as far as possible, similar indignities. So, on 22nd March 1322, just five days after his surrender, the prisoner was mounted on 'a lean white jade without bridle' and led from his grand castle to a nearby hill. His route was lined with villagers who had, in earlier times doffed their cap to the mighty Earl of Lancaster. This time, the peasants jeered and pelted him with earth as he went, unmourned, to his death.

There was no-one there that day to claim Thomas, to grieve for him and have his head sewn back to his body. Certainly not his Countess, Alice, who promptly married her lover. The Earl was buried in Pontefract Priory and then the King and the Despensers began granting his forfeited lands to relations and others whose assistance had helped to bring about the rebel's downfall. The honour of Tutbury was granted to Edward's second son, Prince John.

So, that was the end of Thomas of Lancaster, the most powerful baron that an English King had ever had to contend with. Perhaps the irony of Edward II's situation was that his grandfather Henry III had bequeathed him this problem by granting Thomas's grandfather, Edmund Crouchback, so much land and power in the first place. Certainly, William the Conqueror would never have envisaged that one of his barons - especially such a close relative, would, in return for his castles and his riches, challenge the anointed King.

Afterword

509 years after Thomas fled Tutbury Castle in the face of his cousin Edward's wrath, on Wednesday 1st June 1831, workmen deepening the mill race on the River Dove came across a few silver coins. These were quietly shared out amongst themselves, but over the next few days the river gave up so much coin that it was impossible to offload the booty without intrusive questions being asked. The news of the treasure leaked out and within days the locals were wading chest deep in the river, fishing out this incredible windfall. In one day alone an estimated 20,000 coins were recovered. As none of the coins were dated later than the reign of Edward II it soon became apparent that this cache was the three pay chests of the Earl of Lancaster that had disappeared as he deserted Tutbury Castle. The Duchy of Lancaster eventually took control of the free-for-all and further panning for the coins was forbidden, although it is comforting to think that perhaps villagers whose ancestors suffered the excesses of Thomas's marauding army, back in March 1322, had the chance to fill their boots first.

Edward 2nd of England.   *Alexander of Scotland.*

Coins from the horde discovered in 1831 and dating back to the time of Thomas of Lancaster and Edward II.

John of Gaunt, 2nd Duke of Lancaster. 1340-1399

All that remains of John of Gaunt's Gate. *Courtesy of Dr Roger Joy.*

Chapter 2
A Man of Integrity:
John of Gaunt, Duke of Lancaster

Thomas of Lancaster was not the only noble to die as a consequence of the defeat at Boroughbridge. Sir Robert Clifford who was injured during the siege survived to stand trial. He was hanged alongside his confederate, John Mowbray. In fact, Boroughbridge gave Edward II the chance to have a clearout of his most troublesome barons and by 1323 he had either despatched or imprisoned most of the malcontents who had hitched their wagons to his cousin's star.

But Edward's problems were by no means over now that he had eliminated Thomas and his followers. Having gained complete control of his realm at last, the King immediately caused another upsurge of hostility amongst the thinned-out ranks of his nobility by insisting that the Despensers should remain at his side, wealthy with endowments confiscated from Lancastrian followers. This father and son duo, although not without political ability, were as unpopular as ever amongst the lords. They decided that the King would never have been allowed to hand them so much power if Lancaster had lived - albeit that many of them had deserted the Earl's cause at the eleventh hour! Within a year of his execution, Thomas, who had been forsaken and branded a turbulent troublemaker, became the wronged victim of a feckless King. Miracles were reported to be happening at his tomb and the situation was worrying enough for the Despensers to persuade Edward to post soldiers there as a deterrent to visitors and rabble-rousers.

However, it was not from his nobles that the King's main source of opposition came this time; it was much nearer home. Queen Isabella was no longer the pregnant teenager who Thomas of Lancaster had comforted in Newcastle a decade before. Although she had made an effort to bury the hatchet after Gaveston was removed from the scene, by 1325, in her early thirties and mother of the future King of England, she was not prepared to endure the indignity of her husband's obsession with the younger Hugh Despenser. She made tracks home to France where her brother was now King. There, she met up with one of her husband's enemies, Roger Mortimer of Wigmore, and they became lovers.

Mortimer had sided with Lancaster against Edward in 1321 but his timely surrender towards the end of the year had saved his life and while other nobles suffered execution for their support, he was sentenced to a spell in the Tower of London. Within a year, he had escaped and fled to France from where he and Isabella now planned to invade England.

Naturally, such a plan needed allies in the homeland, nobles who had reason to bear a grudge against the King, so here let me digress just a little..... Years before all this high drama, while Thomas and his brother Henry were youngsters, their father Edmund 'Crouchback' had arranged suitably advantageous marriages for both of them. While Thomas and Alice de Lacy failed to form any sort of useful relationship, Henry and his wife, Matilda de Chaworth, produced six daughters and a son.

A Crown for Staffordshire

THE HOUSE OF LANCASTER

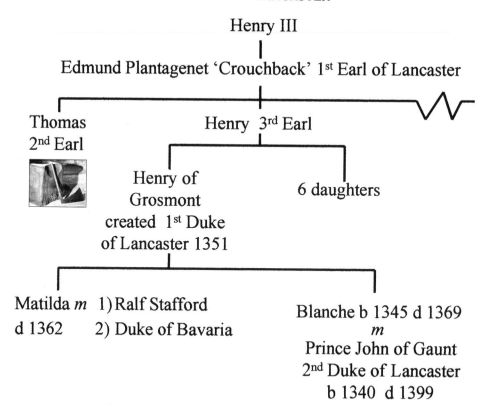

Henry III

Edmund Plantagenet 'Crouchback' 1st Earl of Lancaster

Thomas
2nd Earl

Henry 3rd Earl

Henry of
Grosmont
created 1st Duke
of Lancaster 1351

6 daughters

Matilda *m* 1) Ralf Stafford
d 1362   2) Duke of Bavaria

Blanche b 1345 d 1369
m
Prince John of Gaunt
2nd Duke of Lancaster
b 1340 d 1399

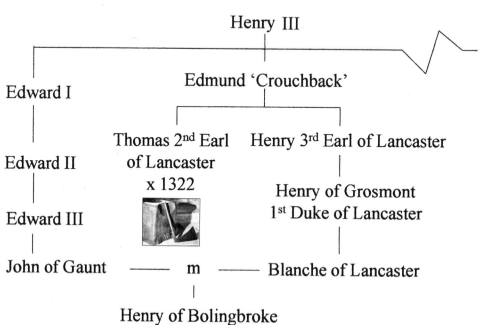

Henry III

Edmund 'Crouchback'

Edward I

Thomas 2nd Earl
of Lancaster
x 1322

Henry 3rd Earl of Lancaster

Edward II

Edward III

Henry of Grosmont
1st Duke of Lancaster

John of Gaunt ——— *m* ——— Blanche of Lancaster

Henry of Bolingbroke
Henry IV

Henry of Grosmont (later 1st Duke of Lancaster) and Edward III were second cousins.
John of Gaunt (2nd Duke of Lancaster) and Blanche of Lancaster were third cousins.

So in March 1322 when Thomas lost his head, Henry, with a son to follow in his footsteps, found himself the dispossessed heir to the great Lancastrian estates. There was a dynasty at stake here and he immediately set about proving that his brother had been illegally put to death, and that his lands should not be forfeit. His claim was based on the fact that Thomas had not been permitted to answer the charge of treason, nor had he been allowed the right to be tried by his peers.

Considering the haste with which Thomas had been despatched, Henry had a very strong case and in March 1324 he was granted one of Thomas's landed titles, the Earldom of Leicester. This, though, was a mere fraction of the immense Lancastrian estates and so Queen Isabella and Mortimer, plotting away in France, found a willing accomplice in Henry Plantagenet.

Other rebels, united in antipathy and jealousy at the favouritism showered on the Despensers, flocked to the Queen's cause when she and Mortimer arrived in England on 24th September 1326 with the clear intention of unseating the King.

London fell very quickly and Edward, with Hugh Despenser the Younger, fled, scouring England for a safe hiding place. On 16th November Henry Plantagenet eventually tracked them down in Neath Abbey, Glamorgan. The King was taken to Kenilworth castle where Henry, to his credit, treated his cousin with respect and consideration. No such lenience was shown to Despenser. He was put on trial within days of being captured and amongst the charges against him was the fact that he had procured the execution of Thomas of Lancaster. His fate was to be hung, drawn and quartered and a contemporary chronicler has left a graphic description of the proceedings, too horrible to be repeated here.

In January of the following year, Henry was among the deputation chosen by Parliament to inform Edward that he had been deposed on account of his incompetence and to ask for his abdication. After a pitiful show of tears, Edward abdicated in favour of his young son, Edward III and henceforth became known as 'the Lord Edward, sometime King of England'. He remained in his cousin Henry's custody, living a reasonably comfortable existence until April, when Isabella and Mortimer seem to have decided that a sterner gaoler was required. His removal from his cousin's care at Kenilworth Castle marked the beginning of the end for Edward as his new gaoler was Thomas de Berkeley. De Berkeley and his father Maurice had fought as Lancastrians at Boroughbridge and been taken prisoners. Later, when Maurice had died in prison, his estates were given to Hugh Despenser. The younger de Berkeley's support for Queen Isabella regained him the family estates and it was at Berkeley Castle that 'the Lord Edward, sometime King of England' met a notoriously hideous death.

Although there is no reason to suspect that Henry ever shared his brother's aspirations of kingship, he certainly took a leading role in ruling England while the fifteen year old Edward III learned the ropes. He was made guardian of his young relative and chief of the Council of Regency. Obviously, in such a position he was nicely placed to reinstate his brother's lost inheritance and within two weeks of the new King ascending his throne, Henry was formally styled Earl of Lancaster and restored to most of the family territories, including the honour of Tutbury.

All seven of Henry and Matilda's children survived the perils of childhood, a

Isabella's forces at Hereford - showing the execution of the
younger Despenser in the background

remarkable achievement in the 14th century, and when the 3rd Earl died in 1345, his only son, known as Henry of Grosmont, inherited the Lancastrian estates. There is no certainty as to precisely when Grosmont was born but he was most probably old enough to understand the situation when his Uncle Thomas was beheaded. The youth would therefore have grown to manhood knowing that in the event of the attainder against his uncle's estates being lifted, he would be heir to the greatest inheritance in the kingdom. By the time he became 4th Earl of Lancaster, Edward III had also grown to manhood and was making a much better job of ruling the country than his father had ever done.

In fact, Henry of Grosmont and the King were cast in the same mould, both clever diplomats and fearless warriors. For services rendered in the Scottish campaigns and in France, Edward created Henry Duke of Lancaster. This was a great honour for dukedoms were normally the perquisite of the sons of kings. In this instance it was understood to have been Henry's reward for his outstandingly loyal and capable services. However, it may also have had something to do with the fact that the King already saw this distant cousin becoming more closely connected to the royal family.

At the time that Henry received his dukedom, he and his wife Isabella had two daughters, aged ten and six. They had no sons. The King on the other hand had five sons and, naturally, he was on the lookout for advantageous marriages. Henry's two daughters, Matilda (Maud) and Blanche, stood to inherit half each of the vast Lancastrian estates, and this, coupled with the fact that their great-grandfather had been Henry III, made them exceedingly marriageable. Grosmont was able to select their husbands from the pick of the nobility. For Matilda he arranged a marriage with Sir Ralph de Stafford's heir, Ralph (Sir Ralph was a close friend of King Edward) but the groom died while Matilda was still a little girl. Before she reached her teens, Grosmont married her to the Duke of Bavaria.

The arrangements for Blanche were not so hurried. She was about fourteen when, in May 1359, she became a royal bride, the wife of King Edward's third son, Prince John of Gaunt. The groom was nineteen and was described as tall and fair, cultured and well educated. Henry of Grosmont had come across his future son-in-law when the Prince was a boy no more than ten years old. It was the occasion of the young Prince John's first battle. He was aboard his elder brother Prince Edward's ship, just off the coast of Sussex, awaiting an invasion of Castilian ships. The Spanish, who were not prepared to accept Edward III's lordship of the seas, sailed into the Channel and engaged the English fleet. Fighting lasted all day and eventually the Castilians were defeated. During the battle, the ship carrying the two princes was involved in a potentially fatal episode. Prince Edward (known later as the Black Prince) had grappled a Spanish vessel, but his crew were unable to clamber aboard and the enemy were getting the upper hand, when Grosmont brought his own ship alongside. With the cry *'Derby to the rescue'* he entered the melee and carried the day.

Snippet Henry of Grosmont, in 1337, was created Earl of Derby - one of the honours that came through the generations from when Henry III confiscated the estates of Robert Ferrers and bestowed them on his son Edmund Crouchback, the founder of the Lancastrian dynasty.

John and Blanche's marriage was a grand affair at Reading Abbey attended by the Kings of England, France and Scotland. By this time, both the bride's and the groom's parents would have felt that Blanche and her sister were certain to succeed to the

Lancastrian inheritance as no male heir had been born to them.

King Edward would have considered this marriage for his third son eminently suitable. Within three years it was to prove even more satisfactory than he could have hoped. Duke Henry and his duchess died of the Black Death in 1361 and the following year their elder daughter Matilda also succumbed to the dreaded disease that had been decimating England since 1348. Twenty-two year old Prince John of Gaunt, by right of his young wife Blanche, came into the whole of his father-in-law's Lancastrian heritage. The dukedom included 31 castles, of which two were Tutbury and Newcastle-under-Lyme, along with a good chunk of north-east Staffordshire.

When John married his heiress, the similarity between his own situation and those of his wife's great uncle, Thomas of Lancaster, must surely have occurred to him. Like Thomas, John had grown up with the crown glittering provocatively near to him. He was born in 1340, the sixth of King Edward and Queen Philippa's thirteen children. Although two of his three elder brothers grew to adulthood, Prince Edward, the heir to the throne, was at twenty nine still unmarried when John married Blanche. Lionel, the heir presumptive had been married for thirteen years, but the union had produced only one child, a daughter. The right of succession through a female was still a grey area never tested since Matilda lost her crown to King Stephen in the 12th century.

So, with wars, famine and the Black Death taking such a heavy toll on life, the crown was as tantalisingly close to John of Gaunt as it had been to Thomas of Lancaster earlier that century. Even after the Black Prince married in 1361, the crown still hovered for another four years until Princess Joan had a boy, Edward. A second son, destined to be Richard II, followed in 1367.

There is insufficient evidence to know whether John and Blanche were happy together. Certainly John had mistresses but his notorious and long term relationship with Katherine Swynford probably did not start until after Blanche's death. John was a fighting man, born in an era when politics were still slugged out on the battlefield and when a king's right to his realm often rested on the strength of his army. This strength could be roughly equated to how much loyalty the king could afford to buy, and the support of the other crowned heads. One political wrangle began when John was just a boy and was to keep him away from his wife and homeland during the latter half of the 1360s, and ultimately shape the rest of his life.

Alfonso, King of Castile and Leon, died in 1350 leaving his sixteen year old son Pedro I to rule over a huge hostile area of Spain. The fact that Don Pedro's father had left him a domain peopled by conquered malcontents was only part of his troubles, for Alfonso had also bequeathed to his son a family of belligerent, illegitimate half brothers. Over the next fifteen years, Don Pedro suffered the unremitting treachery of his eldest half brother Enrique of Trastamara whose attempts to usurp the throne caused continual unrest. Don Pedro lost the friendship and backing of France by marrying Blanche of Bourbon only to desert her the day after for his mistress Maria de Padilla. The French were not impressed, especially as their humiliated princess was forbidden to go home and then suddenly died.

Enrique milked the finer feelings of the French over this incident and so found himself a safe harbour in that country from where he mounted a successful campaign to overthrow

Don Pedro. The ousted Don Pedro wrote for help to Edward III's son the Black Prince who, as Prince of Aquitaine, was living in grand style at his palace in Bordeaux. Without waiting for an answer, Don Pedro trailed his daughters by Maria de Padilla to Bayonne where he learned to his relief that the Black Prince was eager to back his cause.

This was just the sort of scrap that appealed to Edward - to oust the usurper Enrique and reinstate the wronged Don Pedro; never mind the fact that some of his people called him 'Pedro the Cruel'. However, mighty as Prince Edward was in Aquitaine, he still had to send home to his father in England asking for approval before mounting an expedition against Castile.

John of Gaunt, now Duke of Lancaster, was a member of the council who considered the dethroned Castilian King's proposal to unseat Enrique of Trastamare and voted in favour of the project. Shortly afterwards John travelled to his brother in Aquitaine with the necessary Royal Assent. The practicalities of an invasion of Castile were now considered and it became apparent that the King of Navarre would need to be bribed to lead the way through the Pyrenees, and an army of mercenaries needed to be hired. Of course, Don Pedro was completely lacking in funds and the Black Prince, carried away with the notion of this great and gallant undertaking, agreed to lend him the money to finance the army and buy Navarre's compliance.

As surety against repayment of this huge debt, Don Pedro was required to leave his daughters in Bordeaux - which was probably quite a relief for the girls after their exhausting escape from Spain.

John of Gaunt went home to England to raise an army and in November 1366 the Duke returned to France with a thousand men. By February 1367 a huge fighting force was assembled and John led the vanguard of ten thousand troops as they made their way through the treacherous Roncevalles Pass under appalling weather conditions. The next day, the Black Prince, Don Pedro and the bribed King of Navarre followed and on the third day the final column of soldiers came through the pass and spread out on the plains of Pamplona to prepare for the fight ahead of them. The campaign went mainly the invaders' way, and eventually a one-day battle at Najera, on April 3rd, unseated Enrique, and Don Pedro was reinstated as King of Castile and Leon.

It soon became apparent that Don Pedro had no intention of meeting his financial obligation to the Black Prince. Edward and John were forced to hang around in Spain for several months trying to negotiate a settlement while their armies, unpaid and laid low by the unfamiliar climate, were forced to survive by plundering the land they had supposedly come to free from oppression. During this time the first signs of the debilitating illness that was to plague the Black Prince for the rest of his life became apparent. Eventually, having accepted that Don Pedro simply wasn't going to honour his debt, the brothers returned through the Pyrenees and John brought the remains of his army home to England.

The Duke had been away from home for almost a year, during which time his duchess had given birth to her sixth child, Henry. This boy, born at Bolingbroke Castle and thus known as Henry of Bolingbroke, was Blanche's only son to survive. She produced six children between 1360 and 1367, the first while still in her early teens.

The next year John was away at war again - a war brought about in no small part as a

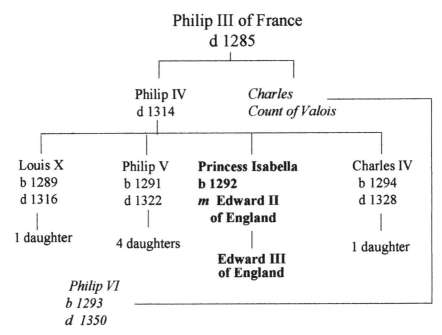

Edward III claimed a right to the French throne through his mother Isabella, the daughter of Philip IV of France.
This claim conveniently ignored the French Salic law which had been used to deny Matilda her throne in 1135.

result of Don Pedro's refusal to honour his debt to the Black Prince. In an attempt to extricate himself from debt, the Black Prince had levied a hearth tax throughout his principality of Aquitaine - a move about as popular as Margaret Thatcher's poll tax of the 1980s. His Gascon subjects saw no reason why they should take financial responsibility for the Prince's war that was, after all, nothing to do with them, and complained to the King of France, who was the Black Prince's overlord in Aquitaine. Charles V accepted the appeal. This, of course, upset the Black Prince who considered the French King to be poking his nose into affairs that were nothing to do with him. Righteous indignation flared up, threats abounded and the ultimate result was that Edward III resurrected his claim to the crown of France by right of his mother, Isabella.

King Charles retaliated by confiscating the Black Prince's French territories and an uneasy peace, which had been established for almost a decade, crumbled into open hostilities, leading to the second epoch of the Hundred Years War.

Things were not working out too well for Don Pedro either. While his English allies started to reap the consequences of their ill thought out decision to assist him, his half brother, Enrique of Trastamara reappeared with French aid to make another assault on the throne of Castile and Leon. There was no chivalrous English contingent to help this time and in March 1369 Enrique routed Don Pedro's unruly, mongrel army.

Realising that the crown was lost, and concerned now merely with survival, Don Pedro sent a message to Trastamara's commander, offering a huge bribe if he were allowed a safe escape. The commander invited the desperate King to his tent, ostensibly to discuss terms. Don Pedro went, only to find that he had been lured into a trap. Enrique was waiting and promptly put a dagger through him.

Meanwhile, the King of France was flirting with the unhappy Gascon nobility, making them grand gifts and promises as he planned to oust the Black Prince from the principality. His plan was to ravage the south coast of England and thus keep the English busy guarding their home while he made inroads into Aquitaine.

John, Duke of Lancaster, was sent to Calais in July 1369 to engage the French and stop them from crossing the Channel. The French refused to do battle and Lancaster ended up marching to Picardy and back to no effect other than the useful spoils of looting.

While he was away in France, the Black Death made its third visitation on England and again it ravaged the house of Lancaster. This time it was Blanche's turn. Possibly weakened after the birth of her last child - not to mention the other six in seven years - the Duchess died on 12th September. She was about twenty-four years old. The Duke, although too busy warring to give much time to grieving, appears to have been mindful of the grand inheritance his wife had brought to him. At the enormous cost of £488 he had a magnificent tomb crafted from the famous Tutbury alabaster. Many years, and two wives, later, his will dictated that he should be laid alongside Blanche. They lay together in Old St Paul's Cathedral, London for more than 260 years, until church and monument were destroyed in the Great Fire of London.

The widowed Duke was fighting in France again the following year, and during the campaign there the wasting disease that had first attacked the Black Prince in the Castilian invasion became debilitating. He was forced to leave John in charge of a struggling Aquitaine and return to England and a lingering death. The night before he sailed for home, his elder son, aged six, died. Edward was too ill to stay for the funeral and the sad task of burying the young boy fell to John.

John struggled on fighting his brother's war and even paid the troops wages from his own resources, until in July 1371 he resigned his Lieutenancy of the principality and went home to England. But he did not return alone. Living off his charity in Bordeaux were Don Pedro's two surviving daughters, Constancia and Isabella. Left there as hostages in 1367, they had proved to be nothing more than an expensive liability. But now it occurred to the Duke, that he, like his brother Edward, could become a king - King of Castile. He had fought successfully in 1367 to cast the usurper Enrique out of Castile for the ungrateful Don Pedro; now he would do it again, and this time he would do it for himself.

In September 1371 he married Don Pedro's seventeen year old heir, Constancia, and became, by right of his bride, John, King of Castile. For Constancia, marriage with the English Prince John, Duke of Lancaster must have been a greatly appreciated reversal of her fortunes. Here was a man of magnificent wealth and importance, son of the great and influential Edward III - and he was going to claim back her kingdom.

> Snippet Within a year of John marrying Constancia of Castile, his brother Edmund married her younger sister Isabella.

So the King and Queen of Castile sailed into Plymouth in November 1371 and Tutbury Castle was chosen from amongst the Duke's many fine residences to be his new bride's palace. He arranged for his children by Blanche to be taken there too, along with their governess, Katherine Swynford.

In the long years since Blanche's great uncle Thomas had abandoned the castle at

Tutbury in his bid to escape Edward II's army, the fortress had remained neglected and partly ruined. Money was lavished on rebuilding and beautifying the place, although little survives of the work carried out and even the surviving gatehouse (now a ruin) known as John of Gaunt's Gate was, in the main, built before he was born.

Constancia lived at Tutbury Castle for a number of years in which time the place took on a distinctly Spanish flavour. The Duchess loved music and singing to such an extent that the Duke caused a Minstrels' Court to be established there which was self-regulating and had the authority to admonish or fine the many musicians who flocked to Tutbury to seek a living.

Tutbury's excruciating bull running custom with its Spanish connotations seems to have come into being during Constancia's time at the castle. The event was held annually and started off benignly enough each year with the election of a new King of the Minstrels, followed by a banquet. After the feast the minstrels, no doubt well oiled with liquor, made their way to the priory gate where crowds had gathered, and a bull was let loose. It was now the task of the minstrels to catch the animal which had been mutilated by the cropping of its horns, ears and tail. Not only that, but the wretched creature's body was smeared with soap and it had pepper blown into its nostrils.

If one of the musicians was brave enough to approach the crazed bull and return to the market square with a few of its hairs, then it was captured and harnessed, and returned to the square where it was baited with dogs. When there was no more fight left in the animal the minstrels were allowed to do as they would with it, either sell it or kill it for food. Incredibly, this hideous custom continued in Tutbury for centuries after its Spanish Queen had been forgotten and its castle had become a tumbled, weed-infested ruin.

For all John permitted Constancia to surround herself with a Spanish Court in Exile, she was, without doubt, a neglected wife. I can't help thinking that this situation had certain compensations for any noble woman of childbearing age in medieval times - she was at least not continually pregnant as her predecessor had been. In fact, John spent so little time with his Spanish consort that the marriage produced only two children, Catalina, in 1372, and Juan in 1374, who died in infancy.

The Duke's neglect of Constancia was probably because by the time he married her he was already deeply involved with Katherine Swynford, the widow he brought to Tutbury as governess to his daughters. Katherine was the daughter of a courtier who had come from Hainault in the retinue of Edward III's wife Queen Philippa back in the 1320s.

> Snippet   Katherine Swynford's sister is thought to have married Geoffrey Chaucer who was for a time employed and patronised by the Duke of Lancaster.

The date of birth of Katherine Swynford's first child by John is not known with certainty so it is impossible to pinpoint when the affair began. Evidence suggests that the child, John, was born between 1371 and 1373, at least fifteen months after Blanche died.

Katherine's duties meant that she lived, from time to time, at Tutbury Castle with Blanche's daughters. It would seem that the Duke paid far more visits to the nursery than he did to his Queen's apartments because the governess bore her employer another three children. These four illegitimate offspring, three sons and a daughter, were given the name Beaufort after one of their father's lordships in France.

Within a year of bringing his Queen to England, John was engrossed in plans for

John of Gaunt Duke of Lancaster

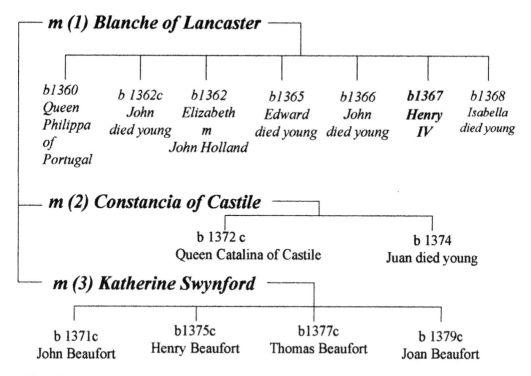

m (1) Blanche of Lancaster

| b1360 Queen Philippa of Portugal | b 1362c John died young | b1362 Elizabeth m John Holland | b1365 Edward died young | b1366 John died young | b1367 Henry IV | b1368 Isabella died young |

m (2) Constancia of Castile

| b 1372 c Queen Catalina of Castile | b 1374 Juan died young |

m (3) Katherine Swynford

| b 1371c John Beaufort | b1375c Henry Beaufort | b1377c Thomas Beaufort | b 1379c Joan Beaufort |

John of Gaunt's families by his three wives. The four children by his mistress Katherine Swynford were made legitimate by Richard II in 1397, though a later charter expressly excluded them from the succession.

another invasion of France. The Black Prince was now too debilitated to take part, so the summer of 1373 found the Duke Commander-in-Chief of as fine an army as England could muster. His remit, at least as far as his father was concerned, was to reverse the losses in France. But John's plans went much further.

As soon as he had married Constancia, in his capacity as King of Castile, he had initiated a correspondence with Fernando I, King of Portugal, and by 1372 these two allies had made a pact to attack Enrique of Trastamara on his Castilian throne.

John now had an army at his disposal and an ally ready and willing to assist him. First, he would cross the Channel and win the crown of France for his father and then he would march his victorious army across the Pyrenees into Castile and with Fernando's help, win the Kingdom of Castile for himself.

Considering that the Duke had not been on a winning side since 1367 when Trastamara had been routed at the battle at Najera (with the Black Prince in control of the tactics) this plan was a dream that John lacked the military flair to fulfil. On his own account the Duke had never won a campaign.

The campaign in France never got off the ground because King Charles played the same game he had played in 1369. Again, the French refused to engage and left John marching up and down without a fight. He marched his army through France from Calais to Bordeaux with little more than the odd skirmish. This incredible journey, although generally bloodless, cost England an army, for the winter march through the Auvergne

Tutbury Church and Castle
from *The History of the Castle, Priory and Town of Tutbury* by Oswald Mosley, 1832.

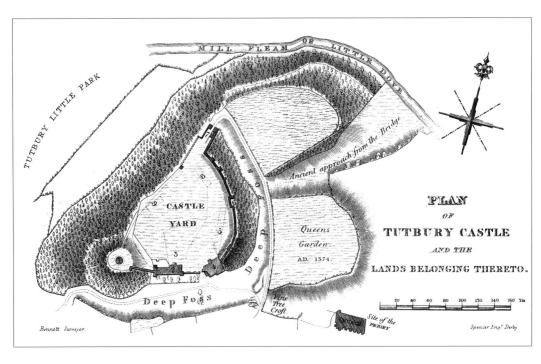

Plan of Tutbury Castle
from *The History of the Castle, Priory and Town of Tutbury* by Oswald Mosley, 1832.

decimated the troops who died from starvation and cold.

By the time the Duke arrived at Bordeaux, instead of a victorious army ready to set off through the Pyrenees and into Spain, he had a dispirited rag-tag of soldiers who took the first opportunity to desert. The dream was over; John arrived home in April 1374 with neither the French crown nor the Castilian one.

Back in England the Duke found himself in a situation that dictated the course of the next decade and left him little time to consider the unseating of Trastamara. The mighty Edward III, now in his early sixties, was drifting into a premature senility, no longer capable of wearing the mantle of Kingship that he had so ably shouldered for over forty years. Queen Philippa had died five years previously and Edward's rapacious mistress, Alice Perrers, was ruling the royal roost.

The Black Prince, at forty-four, was deep in the clutches of his wasting disease and quite obviously not long for this world. By the time his elder son had died he may well have been too ill to father more children, and besides, his wife was also in her forties. The only heir of the senior branch of the Royal House of Plantagenet was the couple's remaining son, Richard of Bordeaux.

John became head of the family, proxying for his enfeebled father and his debilitated elder brother and looking after the interests of his young nephew Richard. This little boy was barely seven years old with a lot of childhood ailments yet to survive. John would have been very well aware that although the Castilian crown had eluded him, the English crown might now fall to him by default.

For the next few years he found himself running the country. It was a thankless task and he was not popular, for the people didn't forgive him the inglorious campaign against France. Compared with the military successes of his father and brother, John was considered a failure. High birth, conspicuous wealth and a lofty, indifferent attitude, did nothing to improve his image, and spiteful rumours about his personal ambitions towards the crown infiltrated court circles. One fantastic story claimed that John was a changeling, smuggled into Queen Philippa's bed because her own baby had died. Now by the time John was born in 1340 the Queen had already provided Edward III with an heir, Edward, and a spare, Lionel (another son William had died in infancy). Furthermore, having been married at fourteen, she was still only twenty-six, with plenty of child-bearing years in front of her. The Queen would have been in no panic to provide her husband with another male heir. The story was a malicious fabrication listened to and perpetrated by men who should have considered it beneath themselves to tittle-tattle.

There was another disagreeable story going the rounds accusing the Duke of murdering his first wife's sister Matilda of Lancaster. He would have been all of twenty-two when he was supposed to have committed this black deed, reputedly to get his hands on the whole of the Lancastrian inheritance.

But the most dangerous rumour, one that John could not ignore, accused him of plotting to kill his nephew Prince Richard so that he could take the throne when the Black Prince died.

That these malevolent stories took hold is a measure of John's unpopularity. Shortly after his brother's painful and lingering end, he took action to seal the slanderers' mouths.

Calling together the great and the good of the land and with the young Prince Richard sitting at the side of the old King, he knelt and swore to accept the boy as sovereign.

This looks very earnest and upright on John's part and indeed, it would seem that he was a man of scruples. The fact remains though, that he had a burning ambition to wear a crown, and while he would not stoop to snatch his young nephew's throne, he was not above taking a crack at it legally. He had, some time before, tried to persuade Parliament to introduce the French Salic law so that, in the event of the Black Prince and his son Richard dying, there could be no claim through Prince Lionel's daughter Philippa. Parliament had refused to play ball, why should they? It was a case of 'if it isn't broken, don't mend it'.... especially as the person who would benefit was the unpopular Duke of Lancaster.

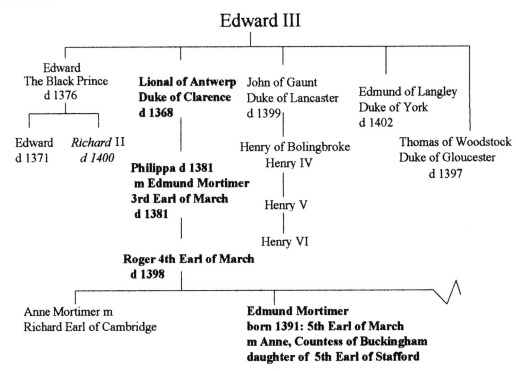

This very simplified family tree shows Edward III's five sons who survived to manhood.
The descendants of Lionel of Antwerp claimed a right to the throne through his only child Philippa.
The descendants of John of Gaunt claimed that the throne could not pass through a female.

The Duke made another attempt to circumvent the line of succession shortly before his father died. He tried to persuade the enfeebled King to name him as his successor in place of Prince Richard. The reasoning behind this suggestion was not without merit or even precedent. At a time when the King was expected to rule over his realm in the true sense of the word, a minor on the throne was bad news and a sure route to civil strife. As for precedent, William the Conqueror himself had named a second son as his heir to the throne of England.

Snippet   William the Conqueror's first son Robert, inherited the lands that his father had inherited and his second son, William II 'Rufus' was bequeathed the lands gained by conquest.

Perhaps, in his poor state of mind Edward now either lacked the ability to bring sound judgement to his decision or was simply not prepared to meddle with the true line of succession. For better or worse, he refused to disinherit his ten year old grandson. He died on 21st June 1377 having outlived his eldest son by just six months. In July, John who was now Edward III's oldest surviving son, organised a grand coronation for Richard II.

During the next eight years the Duke looked after his nephew's interests and protected him against other ambitious magnates who, lacking John's integrity, tried to take advantage of the boy King's inexperience. This huge responsibility meant that the Duke's claim to the throne of Castile was forced to become a secondary consideration. However his ambition did not falter and while Enrique of Trastamara's dynasty passed peacefully to his son Juan I in 1379, Don Pedro's English son-in-law was still addressed in England as 'my lord of Spain' - a fatuous conceit.

At the same time, the crown of England continued to hover close to the Duke's grasp because his nephew's marriage in 1382, when Richard and his bride were both sixteen, failed to produce a male heir - or even a female one.

These were uneasy years for John because King Richard was never quite comfortable with him - which is not surprising since there is no doubt he would have heard of his uncle's attempt to disinherit him when he was too young to argue his corner. Hence, the young man's moods swung dramatically between declaring his uncle a traitor and begging him for help and guidance.

As the King grew into his responsibilities and gathered his own people about him, including an ambitious young man named Robert de Vere, John's position became fraught with danger. De Vere developed a tremendous influence over the King and craftily fanned the flames of suspicion that Richard harboured against his uncle. John had to put up with humiliating public tantrums and outbursts of abuse from his somewhat unstable nephew. On the occasion of creating de Vere, Earl of Oxford, King Richard, who was childless, named Roger, Earl of March, as his heir. Roger's mother was Philippa, the only child of Edward III's second son Lionel, and the claim was only vaild, of course, if it was accepted that the throne could pass through a female .... and so far this had never happened.

King Richard was not alone in his ungrateful outbursts. Court plots to brand John a traitor were numerous, and eventually, after one particularly harrowing experience when De Vere almost managed to have him executed for treason, the Duke withdrew to his castle at Pontefract. There, John could look out at the spot where his first wife's great-uncle had perished as a traitor half a century before and he could see history repeating itself. He was playing the part of Thomas of Lancaster, while De Vere acted the unwise favourite Gaveston, who had set a weak Edward II at odds with his magnates. John decided to keep a low profile and to stay as far away from the political arena as possible.

But even this was not good enough for De Vere who wished the King to be completely rid of the Duke's influence. It was partly this young man's hatred of John that gave 'my lord of Spain' the opportunity to abandon the fraught political scene in England and make war against the usurping House of Trastamara.

Occasionally over the years he had tried to whip up enthusiasm for his Castilian cause, but Parliament had never again taken the bait. Now in the autumn of 1385, circumstances turned in John's favour, as De Vere, doubtless clutching at a chance to rid the Court of the Duke's influence, backed a plea for assistance from King Joao of Portugal who was now at odds with Trastamara's son, King Juan of Castile.

King Juan reckoned he was the rightful King of Portugal, which of course King Joao disputed. English soldiers, particularly the archers, were feared throughout Europe and the Portuguese King sent envoys to England suggesting a combined assault on the troublesome Castilians.

This seemed like a good idea all round: the Duke of Lancaster would get his crown; Queen Constancia would avenge her father's murder; King Joao's realm would be rid of the threat of usurpation; King Richard would be free of his uncle's guiding influence; and De Vere would be top-dog at the English court.

Parliament made finances and troops available and after a grand ceremonial send off when King Richard presented 'King John and Queen Constancia' each with a gold crown to be worn at their Castilian coronation, the quasi-royal entourage set off for Plymouth. From there, on July 7th 1386 the invasion force set sail.

Except for his heir, Henry of Bolingbroke, who stayed at home to guard the Lancastrian interests, John's immediate family accompanied him on the campaign; including Constancia with her daughter Catalina, Duchess Blanche's two daughters Philippa and Elizabeth, and the latter's husband.

Although Lancaster was forty five years old - perhaps past his prime by 14th century standards, he was still a force to be reckoned with, and King Juan of Castile was extremely worried when he heard of the Duke's plans. He sent a secret envoy to John, offering marriage between his elder son Enrique and Constancia's daughter Catalina. John dismissed this - such a settlement would not have put a crown on his head.

Another marriage alliance was deemed to be beneficial to his cause, and so, as a guarantee of an 'all expenses paid' Portuguese army to assist in the fight against Juan of Castile, John married Blanche's elder daughter Philippa to King Joao of Portugal. Thus, a motherless little girl who had been handed over at Tutbury Castle to a neglected Spanish Queen to be reared, became the Queen of Portugal.

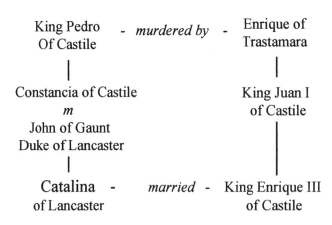

King Pedro Of Castile	- murdered by -	Enrique of Trastamara
|		|
Constancia of Castile m John of Gaunt Duke of Lancaster		King Juan I of Castile
|		|
Catalina of Lancaster	- married -	King Enrique III of Castile

Catalina's father (John of Gaunt) married her to the grandson of the man who had
murdered her grandfather and usurped his throne.
RIGHT: Don Pedro was known both as 'Pedro the Cruel' and 'Pedro the Just'.

Once Philippa and King Joao were married the Castilian campaign began in earnest with a great deal of confidence on the part of 'King John of Castile' and his Portuguese confederates. A formidable enemy was ranged against King Juan and his ally Charles VI of France was giving little more than verbal support. As it turned out, this was enough to win the day, for the French advised Juan to adopt the same tactics they had used against the Duke of Lancaster in 1373. The policy of non-combat worked yet again, for the invaders found no-one to fight. Dispirited by marching in the unaccustomed heat of a Spanish summer and starving for lack of plunder, the once eager soldiery fell victim to dysentery followed by an outbreak of the plague.

'King John's' dream of wearing the crown of Castile was shattered along with his army. Again King Juan approached with the offer of a dynastic marriage alliance between his heir and Don Pedro's grand-daughter. The fact that, with 'King John's' army laid low, Juan was still prepared to offer terms can only mean that the King of Castile was seriously worried about the Lancastrian claim to his throne. This time John accepted the Castilian king's offer of a marriage alliance and in September 1388, two and a half years after leaving England, he married Constancia's sixteen year old daughter Catalina to Enrique of the House of Trastamara. As the groom was only ten years old, the marriage could not immediately be consummated and so it was agreed that Enrique's younger brother would remain unmarried until such time as the groom had fulfilled his marital responsibilities. In the event of his untimely death, then Catalina was to be married to the younger brother.

Snippet   Catalina was great-grandmother of Katherine of Aragon, the first of Henry VIII's wives.

So again, a woman who had spent much of her young life at Tutbury Castle, became a Queen - Queen Catalina of Castile.

As an act of good faith, the Duke gave his rival King Juan the golden crown that had been given him by Richard II. The Duchess Constancia, no longer claiming to be Queen of Castile, returned to England in 1389 to her lonely, quasi-Spanish court, while her husband continued his very public affair with Katherine Swynford.

Constancia died at Leicester Castle in 1394, aged forty. Within two years the Duke, now fifty-six years old, married again. John's previous marriages had been driven by ambition: the first for territorial wealth, the second for a crown. This time, he married to bestow legitimacy upon his four children with Katherine Swynford.

By 1399 the great Duke of Lancaster had outlived most of his contemporaries. His had been a life of overt splendour and exciting adventure even though his ambitions to be a king had been thwarted. But as he neared the end of his days, the crown of England still tantalised him. Roger, Earl of March, the man Richard II had named as his heir, had been slain in battle in 1398, leaving only a young son, Edmund Mortimer. Richard's first wife had died childless and his second wife, Isabella was only ten years old. Would she produce an heir to the throne? In the meantime, what if the King himself was to die? With careful negotiation, could the rights of eight year old Edmund Mortimer, great-grandson of the Duke's long dead elder brother Lionel be side-stepped? Was there still a chance that the English crown might settle peaceably onto a Lancastrian head? Perhaps not for himself now, John accepted that, but for his eldest son Henry Bolingbroke?

Henry Bolingbroke was a great soldier and jouster.

Chapter 3
A Man With No Option:
Henry Bolingbroke, Henry IV

Henry of Bolingbroke grew up as the only legitimate male heir of John of Gaunt, the great Duke of Lancaster. He was born in 1367, the sixth of Blanche of Lancaster's seven children and her fourth son. His three elder brothers died in infancy and later, when his stepmother Constancia of Castile bore a son, he too died very young.

So Henry grew up knowing that he was, in his father's eyes at least, a very special person who would in the fullness of time inherit the fabulous riches of the Duchy of Lancaster and perhaps would be in direct line for the throne of England

His father was the third of Edward III's five sons who had lived to marry and have children. By the time Henry was eleven two of his uncles had died: Prince Edward, the Black Prince, who had been heir to the throne, and the King's second son, Prince Lionel. This left the Duke of Lancaster as the eldest living son. Henry's cousin, Prince Richard, was the only surviving child of Prince Edward and heir to the throne, but he was a frail specimen, not made of the same stuff as his fearsome father or his gallant grandfather. If Richard died, the Duke of Lancaster would become heir to the throne and so, ultimately would Henry.

There was just one glitch. Prince Lionel had a daughter Philippa who had borne a son, Roger Mortimer. With no law of succession, Roger's indirect claim to the throne through his mother was every bit as open to argument as Henry's direct claim through his father.

When Henry was two years old his mother fell victim to the plague. Two years later his father remarried, and his new bride, Constancia of Castile, chose to live at Tutbury Castle at first. Henry and his two sisters were taken there. These Tutbury years were idyllic, for the little boy was surrounded with young women and children. Besides Constancia and her daughter Catalina, there was a widowed governess who brought with her two children from her own marriage and an illegitimate son named John. This was Katherine Swynford, and the father of her bastard child was Henry's father, John of Gaunt.

We are talking about a 'menage à trois' here, where, it seems, the wife and the mistress lived amicably and the children were shared. Perhaps it worked because the Duke of Lancaster was so busy looking after the interests of his senile old father, Edward III, his ailing brother, Prince Edward and his highly strung young nephew, Prince Richard.

This tranquil interlude in young Henry's life was not to last. When Prince Edward lost the fight with his terrible illness in 1376, the boy was catapulted out of Tutbury Castle's petticoat kingdom into a far more earnest environment. He was selected by his grandfather as a companion for the new heir to the throne, Prince Richard. He was vested with one of his father's titles, the Earl of Derby, and packed off to Kennington Palace to live, learn and play with his cousin, along with other suitable youngsters of high birth, including Robert de Vere, Ralph Stafford and Thomas Mowbray.

Snippet   This Thomas Mowbray was the great-grandson of John Mowbray who joined forces with Thomas of Lancaster and came to grief in Edward II's 1322 cull of troublesome barons.

Henry's father spent most of his time at court and having his son at Kennington meant that he was able to exert a great deal more influence over him than would have been possible if the boy had remained under the gentle Tutbury regime. Perhaps the young, fatherless Richard resented Lancaster's affection and support for Henry. He certainly grew to resent his uncle's presence and considered him to be interfering and manipulative - which, of course, the Duke was, but only with the most honourable of intentions.

There is little evidence to suggest that Henry found any great pleasure in his cousin Richard's company for all that they were thrust together at such an early age. In fact, during the years when a bond of love and loyalty might have been forged between them, several incidents occurred which could hardly have left Henry feeling any good will towards his cousin. In June 1381 the peasants, who were staggering under the burden of a new poll tax introduced by the Chancellor Archbishop Simon Sudbury, rebelled against their lot and converged on London. Richard, who by this time had succeeded his grandfather to the throne as Richard II, fled to the safety of the Tower of London with his friends and relations, and the ministers who the mob declared had misled him.

The Duke of Lancaster, the most powerful and wealthy of the magnates, was top of the mob's 'hit list', but, because he was in Scotland they had to content themselves with burning down his London home, the Savoy Palace, and slaughtering a few of his retainers. Henry was obviously in great danger, especially with his conspicuous red hair, so, when it was decided that the King and his closest courtiers should ride out from the Tower to meet the peasants and attempt to calm them down, Henry was not allowed to go with them.

There was no doubt in the minds of those left behind in William the Conqueror's old fortress, that if the King (who was only fourteen years old) did not manage to come to terms with the mob, none of them were likely to see out the day. The peasants demanded that Richard should abolish serfdom and do away with the ruling classes. They insisted that he should rule them directly and without the financial burden of an expensive baronial class who were ultimately supported by the sweat of the labouring multitudes. They called for the heads of those they considered corrupt or traitorous and Richard, surrounded by a mob of irate peasants, more or less agreed to their demands. Reports as to what the young King actually agreed to are confused - at best he gave them permission to catch those they considered traitors and bring them to him to be punished. At worst, he gave them carte blanche to put these men to death. Whatever he did or did not say, the peasants seem to have interpreted his words to mean that they could storm the Tower

In the meantime, back in the Tower, Simon Sudbury gathered together Henry and others who were at real risk from the rebels. In his capacity as Archbishop of Canterbury, he took his frightened flock into the chapel of St John in the White Tower where he heard their confessions and prepared them to meet their maker. The marauders eventually broke into the sanctuary and Henry, Sudbury and several others were hauled away to Tower Hill for execution. In the horror and confusion of the slaughter, Henry's life was saved when one of the rebellion's leaders protected him from an assailant's weapon.

Snippet   In 1400, within four months of Henry usurping the throne, a plot to murder him and his four young sons was unearthed. Amongst the conspirators was John Ferrour who had refused to allow the mob to kill the young Henry during the 1381 Peasants Rebellion - presumably because of his tender years. Now Henry repaid his debt by granting Ferrour a free pardon.

St John's Chapel in the White Tower, Tower of London

So Henry survived to put a sixty one year blip in the royal succession, but many of the men he knew, including Archbishop Sudbury and his father's surgeon, were butchered on Tower Hill that day.

King Richard rode out again the next day and persuaded his unruly subjects to disperse. For this act of bravery he was, quite justifiably, acknowledged as a hero. Henry's memories of the 1381 Peasants' Rebellion though, would always be tinged with the knowledge that his cousin had been prepared to hand him over to the mob.

By this time, Henry had been married for about a year. His father had provided him with a suitably wealthy heiress, Mary de Bohun who was due to inherit half of the Earl of Hereford's estates. In fact, she was destined to become a nun until Lancaster decided that her financial assets were too good to miss. To forestall the plans already made for little Mary and to obtain her hand for his son, the Duke had to pay Richard II 5,000 marks. The bride was just eleven years old, and it was agreed that the couple would not cohabit for another three or four years. However, it seems that Henry was keen to exercise his marital prerogative, and young Mary appears hardly to have discouraged him, because she produced their first child when she was twelve years old. The baby boy died very shortly after he was born.

Marriage did not interfere with the strong father-son relationship between Henry and his father, and the Duke kept a watchful eye over him. He indoctrinated his heir with an innate loyalty to the King and an acknowledgement of the responsibilities that his privileged high-born status brought.

Richard, egged on by Robert de Vere, viewed his uncle with suspicion and resented his political presence. So together they set up a rather crude and ill thought out ploy to have Lancaster accused of plotting Richard's murder. When a Carmelite friar told Richard his uncle was planning to assassinate him, the King, now seventeen years old and no less unstable than he had been as a boy, immediately ordered the Duke's execution. Fortunately for Lancaster, there were cooler heads about and the King was persuaded that an investigation into the facts was needed before the Duke was made to die.

Although the Carmelite friar was tortured to death, no satisfactory evidence against Lancaster surfaced, probably because there was none. There is nothing on record to tell us how young Henry felt about this sinister affair. We can assume, though, that his position at Richard's court would have been getting isolated by this time. He would have been acutely aware that once again the King had been prepared to feed a Lancastrian to the wolves.

The next year Richard and de Vere were joined by Thomas Mowbray, another of the youngsters who had grown up at Kennington, in an even more blatant attempt to remove Henry's father from his position as chief political adviser. The plan was to summons Lancaster to a meeting of the King's council, seize him as soon as he appeared and charge him with treason. A bench of judges, aware of what their verdict had to be, was hand picked and awaiting their victim.

This time failure was not due to a lack of thoroughness on the part of the conspirators, but a matter of too many people in the know. The conspiracy leaked out and the Duke refused to attend the meeting. He did, however, turn up at the King's palace a few days later dressed in his chain mail and escorted by several hundred armed men. He gave his nephew a thorough dressing down and made it clear that he would go to no more council meetings until the men who had plotted his downfall were dealt with.

Although Richard meekly heard out his uncle and promised to take notice, no retribution was taken against de Vere and Mowbray. Once again young Henry watched the King turn his back on his Lancastrian kinsmen. And later that year Henry witnessed another display of his cousin's paranoid mistrust of the Duke when trouble with Scotland brought the nobles out in force to defend England. This was the only occasion when Richard led an invasion force, and Lancaster, who had retreated to his castle at Pontefract after the attempt on his life, loyally turned up with an army to support his King.

Snippet   This invasion got off to a bad start because a brawl broke out near York and Richard II's half brother, Sir John Holland, slaughtered Ralph Stafford. Ralph was the son of the Earl of Stafford and had grown up as one of young Richard II's companions. The King was so upset about the death of his close friend that he insisted Holland should be tried and punished as a commoner. This threat, at a time when wealth and class could buy immunity for the odd indiscretion upset Princess Joan - the mother of both Richard II and John Holland, to such an extent that she died in utter distress a few months later.

The Duke, a seasoned campaigner whose forces represented a third of the total army, proposed a tactical move which Richard, egged on by de Vere, spurned. The King publicly accused his uncle of being a traitor to the cause and then ordered a retreat, the opposite of Lancaster's suggested tactics.

Such outbursts against the Duke would have been painful and humiliating for young Henry to bear, but Lancaster had reared him to respect his cousin as King, even if respecting him as an individual was out of the question. In the name of loyalty, Henry was forced to remain close to the cousin he despised.

At this point, when it was obvious that there could be no accord between Richard and his uncle, Parliament voted Lancaster the funds to mount his long anticipated campaign in Castile. This had the effect desired by Richard and his friends of distancing the Duke from the English political scene. From Plymouth, on a summer's day in 1386, crowds witnessed a mass exodus of the House of Lancaster, as the Duke and his family set sail to right the wrongs done to his Spanish Queen and win the Castilian crown. Henry accompanied his father's splendid retinue to the docks, and there he bade farewell to Queen Constancia, the stepmother who had reared him at Tutbury, his two sisters Philippa and Elizabeth, and his half sister Catalina. It was considered a vital precaution that Henry remained in England to protect the Lancastrian interests.

> Snippet   Also in the Castilian campaign party was Elizabeth's new husband John Holland, the same man who had killed Ralph Stafford a few months before. No doubt this young man was extremely glad of an excuse to get out of England and give King Richard time to cool his wrath.

With the Duke of Lancaster absent, the King continued to overspend and misgovern until a threatened invasion by the French brought the situation to a head. Two of the country's most experienced military commanders, Thomas of Woodstock, Duke of Gloucester, and Richard FitzAlan, Earl of Arundel, stalwarts from the previous reign, were passed over in favour of de Vere and Michael de la Pole, a couple of military lightweights.

> Snippet   Thomas of Woodstock (Plantagenet), Duke of Gloucester, was Edward III's youngest son, brother of the Black Prince and John of Gaunt. He was therefore uncle to both Henry of Bolingbroke and Richard II.

As it happened, Richard's decision not to place the kingdom's defence in the hands of his expert warlords, was of no consequence because the French invasion never actually took place but the incident paved the way for political upheaval. When Richard asked Parliament to raise taxes for a war chest against a suspected onslaught by the French the following year, Gloucester and Arundel took the opportunity to insist that no money should be granted until the King agreed to an overhaul of his spending policies.

During this confrontation, Henry kept his head down like the loyal subject his father had taught him to be. In the middle of these serious negotiations Richard chose to further the wealth and status of de Vere by creating him Duke of Ireland. It must have been galling for Henry to see his cousin elevate the man who had helped plot to destroy his father.

Richard refused to cooperate with Gloucester and Arundel, even though they had the backing of the Lords and the Commons. The two magnates then threatened to depose him, quoting from an ancient statute that stated they were within their rights if the King refused the 'wholesome advice of the lords and peers'.

The King reluctantly agreed to the setting up of a baronial council to control the government and to the dismissal of his chancellor, de la Pole. But, smarting under the weight of his shackles, the King embarked on an outwardly innocuous royal progress. In fact, this tour of the counties gave him and de Vere opportunity to raise an army.

The King now outlawed Gloucester, Arundel and their supporters on the grounds that the Control Council they had imposed was illegal. A proclamation to this effect was drawn up and signed by several eminent justices. Worse, it also stated that everyone who had backed the lords in their decision to fetter the King was guilty of treason and could look forward to a traitor's death. This fearsome threat brought an older, more venerable and experienced nobleman to join Gloucester and Arundel. He was Thomas Beauchamp, Earl of Warwick, a man in his early fifties who had been in his younger days a companion of Edward III and a founder member of the Order of the Garter.

Snippet Thomas Beauchamp, Earl of Warwick was the grandson of Guy Beauchamp, the Earl of Warwick who kidnapped Edward II's favourite, Piers Gaveston, back in 1312.

These three began to gather their armies about them while Richard finished his royal progress. When he returned to London, without the army he had been busily raising, he found his city under siege. Gloucester, Arundel and Warwick were very careful to let Richard know that they had not armed themselves against their King and they were not traitors, rather, they had come to warn him about the traitorous company he kept. They demanded that five members of his retinue including de Vere and de la Pole be tried for high treason.

Henry, throughout these extraordinary goings on played it cool, mindful no doubt that his father was unlikely to be pleased to come home and find his heir at loggerheads with the King and involved in accusations of high treason.

Richard, with no army on hand and the city menaced with enemy soldiers was forced to agree to the demands of these three powerful lords, who had given themselves the title Lords Appellant. He promised that he would deliver his friends for trial before Parliament the following February. The Lords Appellant, delighted with the outcome of their highly dubious treatment of the King, dismissed their troops and went off to spread the good news that Richard's mischievous councillors were to be put on trial.

They misjudged their King completely. Instead of keeping his friends under house arrest as he had promised, he allowed several of them to escape abroad, while de Vere scurried off to collect the army assembled during the recent royal progress. It was not long before the Lords Appellant learned that the King had broken his promise and that de Vere was marching south with an army. They again mustered their troops, but this time their ranks were swollen with two extra retinues. Henry could sit on the fence no longer. The chance of doing battle with de Vere, the man who had twice endangered his father's life, was more than he could ignore. With him, to the Appellants' rallying point at Huntingdon, marched Thomas Mowbray, another of Richard's hand-picked, childhood friends. Mowbray had remained one of the King's closest friends, but after marrying the daughter of the Earl of Arundel without royal permission, he had suddenly found himself out of favour.

De Vere was no match for the accumulated military experience of the Lords Appellant. As he marched his army southwards through the Cotswolds, his enemies funnelled him towards a route across the upper Thames and thus into a neatly laid trap. The inept young commander led his troops through Burford to Radcot Bridge where Henry's men, having weakened the bridge by sawing through several of its supports, lay waiting, hidden in swirling, winter mists.

De Vere had raised his army by telling the men that they were to fight in Ireland. They had no heart to slaughter their fellow Englishmen in what they saw as nothing but a private quarrel between the barons. They fled, leaving de Vere to escape into the murky night, never to be seen in England again.

Henry was now a fully initiated member of the Lords Appellant and he made his way with Gloucester, Arundel, Warwick and Thomas Mowbray to the Tower of London where Richard had fled for safety. They seized the keys to the great wooden gates and raised the portcullises, then, cut off from the outside world, they began to discuss with the King what his fate was to be.

It now emerged that the three original Appellants had more in mind than simply destroying the councillors who had persuaded Richard to declare them traitors. Henry suddenly found himself embroiled in a discussion to depose the King and replace him with Gloucester. He objected. His uncle, Gloucester, was the fifth and youngest of Edward III's sons, whereas Henry's own father was the third and therefore had a stronger claim to the throne. In any case, even had Gloucester's claim been valid, Henry's upbringing was far too steeped in loyalty to go along with such a scheme. Arming against 'false councillors' in order to protect the King was a dangerous undertaking, hovering precariously on a careful interpretation of the law, but to depose the King was out and out treachery. Henry would be no party to it.

The Appellants were in danger of falling apart but for their own safety, they had to remain as a united force and so the King was allowed to keep his crown. His powers, though, were vested in the five Lords Appellant whose next move was to destroy the men who had endangered their lives by persuading Richard to declare them traitors. During the next months, Gloucester, Arundel, Warwick, Thomas Mowbray and Henry presided over a witch-hunt and blood letting that was dubbed the 'Merciless Parliament'. Richard was stripped completely of his friends - men considered by the new regime to be the traitors who had given him bad advice and persuaded him to overspend. The King sat through the ordeal, unable to save the lives of his friends who had not managed to flee the country. He was not even allowed to save his sick old tutor, Sir Simon Burley. Henry, like Richard, had known this frail, gentle man since he was a boy and he too pleaded for his life but Parliament was not in the business of compassion. Burley was dragged away to be executed on Tower Hill.

Henry, as one of the Lords Appellant, ruled the kingdom throughout 1388 and perhaps it was at this time that he first discovered a taste for power. It was short lived though, because in May 1389 Richard became of age. He declared he would rule without the aid of his Council of Regency and dismissed the Lords Appellant.

By this time the Duke of Lancaster had sewn up his Castilian campaign and married off his two daughters. He was able to make hasty tracks for England when Richard, with more than a hint of panic, ordered him to. It seems that the King had at last come to realise that his uncle was indeed a loyal advisor whose purpose over the years had only been to protect him from less scrupulous individuals.

The Duke must have been greatly disappointed as well as exceedingly anxious when he learned of his son's involvement with the Appellants. Lancaster, of course, had known Richard since birth and had watched him grow to manhood struggling with an unstable personality and an oversized ego. In fact, during Henry's and Richard's formative years, the Duke had spent more time in his nephew's company than in his son's and he was keenly aware of the King's inclination to paranoia.

There is no doubt that Lancaster had real fears for Henry's life especially while he remained at court. On the basis of 'out of sight, out of mind', the Duke arranged for his heir to leave England. Henry's extended 'holiday' took the best part of three years. He jousted in France, crusaded against the infidel in Lithuania, and finally made a pilgrimage to Jerusalem. In between he came home just long enough to celebrate the birth of his latest child or impregnate Mary with the next one.

While he was away, Richard, with the Duke at his side, made every effort to rule peaceably and gain the respect and loyalty of his advisors and the love of his subjects. He accepted Gloucester, Arundel and Warwick back into court circles and Thomas Mowbray regained his former niche as one of his closest friends and councillors. By the summer of 1393, when Henry finished his grand tour of the Holy Land and made his leisurely way home, he found an affable King seeking the company, advice and support of the ex-Appellants. There seemed no inkling of a grudge against the men who had been traitorous and Henry may well have felt that his father had over-reacted by insisting on his removal to foreign parts.

However, an incident the next year was to reaffirm John of Gaunt's foreboding and again rock Henry's faith in his cousin. One of the King's personal knights was discovered to be plotting to murder Henry, his father and his uncle Gloucester. Henry and Lancaster examined the plotters and dealt with them, while the ringleader, Sir Thomas Talbot, was handed over to the King for punishment. They were deeply concerned when they learned that Richard, instead of having Talbot executed, had sent him to the Tower for a brief spell. Even though they complained bitterly to Richard about the leniency of the sentence, the King turned a deaf ear and later granted the man a pardon and re-employed him. This was the first of several incidents that kept Henry and the other ex-Appellants on edge, never quite sure what Richard was thinking. Were they forgiven, or weren't they? It's possible that their mercurial King didn't quite know himself.

The next year three deaths in very quick succession left Henry, his father and the King all widowers within three months of each other. Henry's step-mother Constancia of Castile died in March, releasing the Duke of Lancaster from a marriage of convenience. In early June, Richard's Queen died, a victim of the plague. Although they had been married for twelve years and from all accounts were very fond of each other, Anne was childless. It is generally considered that she was barren but the many rumours of Richard's sexual inclinations may mean that he never gave her the opportunity to provide England with an heir, especially bearing in mind that he did not have any illegitimate children either.

During the week when the Queen died, Henry's wife gave birth to her seventh child, a daughter. After the birth of her first baby when she was twelve years old, Mary had not conceived again for five years. Simple arithmetic means that her next six children were born in just seven years. She lived for only four days after this seventh birth. The child,

Philippa, survived and was reared with her siblings by a stream of foster parents in a variety of grand residences including, from time to time, Tutbury Castle.

While Henry, with four sons, was under no great pressure to marry again, his cousin still had a nation waiting for him to provide them with an heir to the throne. Although Richard was devastated by the loss of his Queen, he recognised her death as the opportunity to further his peace policy with France by a suitable marriage. Such a peace plan for the cash-strapped kingdom was farsighted, sensible and ambitious, though not altogether popular amongst those who equated peace with unemployment. Fighting the French had kept many in work for the past two generations. The burghers and traders who realised that peace would reduce taxes were more in sympathy with the idea, whilst the Lords were divided - Henry and his father were definitely pro-peace, while two of the old Appellants, Gloucester and Arundel were noisily anti-peace.

The Duke of Lancaster was given the delicate task of negotiating with Charles VI of France for the hand of his daughter, Princess Isabella. In November 1396 Henry was part of the entourage who accompanied the King to Calais and witnessed the French King hand his daughter over to her new husband. The King was 29 years old; his bride was eight.

Henry was now closely linked to four dynasties: his sister was married to the King of Portugal, his half sister to the King of Castile, his cousin was the King of England and his cousin's wife was the daughter of the King of France. To top off this pedigree, his father had been granted the Duchy of Aquitaine as part of the French peace process. There was no man in the kingdom with greater connections or expectations than Henry of Bolingbroke.

During the long years of Richard's first marriage it became an accepted fact that Queen Anne was not going to bear children. The King had named his Uncle Lionel's grandson Roger Mortimer as his heir, but never since the Conquest had anyone so distantly related to the King succeeded to the throne. While Richard had no direct heirs, Henry, as his first cousin could still perhaps dream of a crown. But now there was a new queen and although it would be some years before the King could take her to his bed, Henry had to accept that there was every prospect of royal babies.

Richard's new bride brought with her a 28 year peace treaty that released the King from his continual quest for war finances. The promise of a long peace brought reduced taxes and a more affable and pliant kingdom so, at last, Richard had the time to turn his attention to settling long festering scores against the men who in 1388/89 had caused his humiliation and torment.

The opportunity to begin a systematic programme of revenge occurred in the summer of 1397 when the King learned that Gloucester, Arundel and Warwick had dined together at Arundel Castle. This intelligence gave him the excuse to have the three Lords arrested on the grounds of plotting a new treason. There were vague reports that Henry and Mowbray were also at Arundel Castle that evening, but Mowbray had shown himself to be so much Richard's man that it seems highly unlikely that anybody hatching a plot against the King would have invited him.

With Henry the situation was less clear. Since his liaison with the Appellants, Richard had never entirely trusted his cousin even though the Duke of Lancaster had worked ceaselessly to build bridges between the two young men. But Henry was no fan of his uncle

Gloucester, who was doggedly set against the French alliance, and it is hard to accept that, with his father close at hand, Henry would have allowed himself to take part in any scheme against the Crown.

Whatever Richard believed of the rumour concerning his two childhood companions, this was not the time to show his hand because he needed their help in his plan of retribution. He chose to ignore that particular piece of information whilst the three older men were rounded up and imprisoned. Warwick was sent to Tintagel Castle in Cornwall, Arundel to Carisbrooke Castle on the Isle of Wight and the King's uncle, Gloucester, under the care of Mowbray, was taken to Calais.

The arrests caused more than a flutter of concern in high places and even if Mowbray at this point felt secure in his friendship with the King, Henry must have winced with anxiety. When would it be his turn? How long would he last when his politically powerful father died? The Duke of Lancaster was in his late fifties and there were signs that his health was deteriorating.

A trial date of 17th September was set to hear these supposed treasonable offences. The King was determined that Parliament would bring in the verdict he wanted against his old tormentors and Mowbray was one of eight new Appellants selected to prepare charges against the men. Henry was to play his part in the downfall of his old comrades as well by attending the trial proceedings with his armed retainers, who were to act, if required, as backup to Richard's own 2,000 archers.

A few days before Parliament opened it was learned that Gloucester had died in France. Whispers suggested that he had been murdered, a fact that would not so much have surprised Henry as petrified him. It was obvious that the accusations to be aired during the imminent proceedings would not stand the light of a fair trial and so his uncle had been silenced rather than allowed to answer for himself.

His anxiety was confirmed when Parliament opened with the Chancellor informing the assembly that the King's general pardon, granted after the Merciless Parliament of 1388, was annulled. In other words, the four surviving Appellants and everyone else, Lords, clergy and burgesses who had backed them all those long years before, were now deemed to be traitors and were to be made answerable to the law.

Henry's youthful act of disloyalty to the Crown had finally come home to roost, just as his father had feared. To save his skin, Henry gave damning evidence against Arundel. He related that when he first joined the Appellants at Huntingdon, the Earl had suggested they should depose the King. Arundel denied the allegation, but it made no difference to the fate Richard had planned for him and later that day he was taken to Tower Hill and beheaded.

This was not all that was required of Henry. A confession signed by Gloucester while he was Mowbray's prisoner in Calais was produced. This document related how the Appellants had agreed to depose the King and Henry went along with the decision to brand his uncle posthumously a traitor.

Next it was Warwick's turn. The old Earl had spent most of the last ten years at his Castle in Warwick, well out of Richard's way. This seems to have paid off because Richard agreed that instead of execution, he would suffer the lesser punishment of forfeiture and banishment to the Isle of Man.

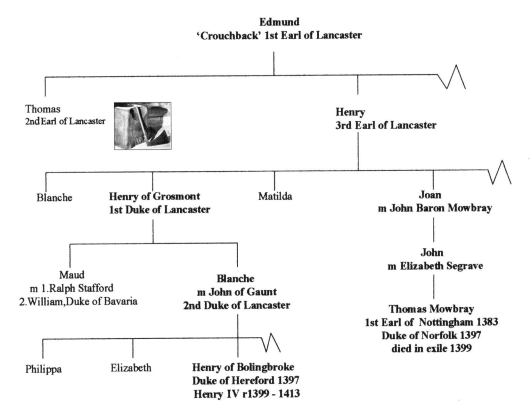

Edmund
'Crouchback' 1st Earl of Lancaster

Thomas
2nd Earl of Lancaster

Henry
3rd Earl of Lancaster

Blanche

Henry of Grosmont
1st Duke of Lancaster

Matilda

Joan
m John Baron Mowbray

John
m Elizabeth Segrave

Maud
m 1.Ralph Stafford
2.William,Duke of Bavaria

Blanche
m John of Gaunt
2nd Duke of Lancaster

Thomas Mowbray
1st Earl of Nottingham 1383
Duke of Norfolk 1397
died in exile 1399

Philippa

Elizabeth

Henry of Bolingbroke
Duke of Hereford 1397
Henry IV r1399 - 1413

At the end of the day, the King repaid the loyalty of those who had helped him achieve this most satisfactory result in his usual way - he handed out titles and grants. Henry was created Duke of Hereford and Mowbray, Duke of Norfolk.

Henry knew though, that the granting of a dukedom was no proof of his cousin's sincerity. After all, Richard had created their uncle Duke of Gloucester - and now the man was dead, most likely murdered with the complicity of his benefactor. The new Duke of Hereford had done everything that Richard had asked of him to prove his loyalty - he had helped send Arundel to his death, he had done his share in banishing Warwick and he had agreed to the besmirching of his uncle's name. He could do nothing more; he could only wait and hope that he had done enough. He had not long to wait.

Just three months later, Henry and the newly created Duke of Norfolk were riding together towards London when Mowbray told Henry that the King had not forgiven them for their role as Appellants. He said that there was a plot to murder Henry, his father and Mowbray himself. He also said that Richard was considering reversing the judgement against Thomas of Lancaster, a move that could have grave financial implications for both of them. Mowbray suggested that they plan a counter-action.

Snippet Thomas of Lancaster was great, great uncle to both Henry of Bolingbroke and Thomas Mowbray. When Thomas of Lancaster was executed for treason in 1322 Edward II confiscated his estates, but later the dead earl's brother Henry 3rd Earl of Lancaster successfully argued that this judgement was unsound and recovered the inheritance.

Henry went immediately to the King and repeated the conversation. Exactly why he chose this course of action is unclear. Was it self preservation? Was he trying to cover his back? If Mowbray, acting on Richard's instructions was attempting to entice him to treason, then his best bet was to pull the rug from under the pair of them by getting his version of the conversation to the King first. Was it revenge? Did Henry see Mowbray's talk of counter-action as the chance to take vengeance against the man who had custody of his murdered uncle of Gloucester? If Richard and Mowbray were not setting him up, then reporting the conversation to the King would show that Mowbray had treachery in mind.

Richard was, or at least appeared to be, alarmed at the story and called for the two men to appear in court. The Dukes flung accusations at each other and eventually, as there were no independent witnesses, the matter was referred to a Court of Chivalry. At this hearing, the aggrieved parties refused to resolve their differences and so the King, with apparent reluctance, appointed a day for a trial by combat. The date set was 16th September, which happened to be the anniversary of the Duke of Gloucester's murder.

Trial by combat, with its belief in divine intervention to assure a victory for the innocent party, was already, in the late 14th century, an outmoded method of justice. People had come to accept that the outcome had more to do with prowess than innocence or guilt. However, plans went ahead and in due course the pageant with all its pomp and colourful ceremony began. The King and his nobles watched and just as Henry started his advance down the lists towards Mowbray, Richard threw down his staff. The dramatic intervention meant that the King was prepared to take matters into his own hands and pass judgement rather than allow the protagonists to fight to the death.

For the next two hours the anxious contestants and disappointed spectators waited while the King and his councillors deliberated. When their verdict was delivered, the spectators - who had already lost their sport - proclaimed it to be neither fair nor rational. Both men were to be banished from the kingdom as traitors, Mowbray for life and Henry for ten years. But in a move completely alien to a conviction for treachery the King agreed to allow his cousin to retain his estates and receive an income from them. Richard also promised that if Lancaster died while Henry was still in exile, then the estates would pass from father to son without intervention. A promise that Richard, to his peril, would see fit to break.

Mowbray, who was popularly considered to be the villain of the whole episode, set off on a pilgrimage to Jerusalem and died a broken man within the year. Henry, on the other hand, had his exile reduced to six years even before he left England. After a tremendous send-off, he went straight to the court of Charles VI of France where he was treated as a welcome and important guest, at least until the Earl of Salisbury was sent on a mission to Paris and put everybody in the picture. Salisbury snubbed Henry and referred to him as a traitor. It was all very embarrassing for Henry, especially as plans for him to marry the French king's cousin were immediately dropped.

While still at the French court, and dallying with the idea of a crusade to fill in an idle year or so, news came to Henry that his father was dying. The Duke of Lancaster had spent the last ten years trying to shield his son from the legacy of his youthful treachery. He died in February 1399 without seeing Henry. At the time of his Uncle's death, Richard was busy planning to take an army to Ireland. His representative there, Roger Mortimer, had been killed in a skirmish the previous year and the King felt it important to take a force over and bring this unsettled part of his kingdom to heel. The cost of financing an expedition was a tremendous burden and Richard, who was notoriously profligate, saw the death of his uncle as an opportunity to ease his problems. He decided to annex the Duchy of Lancaster to the crown, using the excuse that the original decision to allow Henry, as a traitor, to retain his inheritance was contrary to the law.

> **Snippet** Roger Mortimer's murder in 1398 left his eight years old son Edmund as heir to the English throne. This meant that if Richard II met an untimely death the country would be in for another spell with a minor on the throne - a serious problem at a time when the lack of a strong king meant civil strife as the nobles jostled for power.

The move had the added attraction of impoverishing and weakening Henry who still enjoyed a great deal of popularity - not to mention sympathy -in his homeland. Henry learned in May that his inheritance had been seized and that the King was feverishly redistributing Lancastrian estates amongst his friends and relations. The home of his most carefree childhood years, Tutbury Castle, had been allocated to Thomas Holland, the son of Richard's half brother of the same name. Lincoln Castle went to the Duke of Aumale who was Richard and Henry's cousin, the son of Edmund, Duke of York. Henry's brother-in-law, the troublesome John Holland who a dozen or so years before had been threatened with trial as a commoner for the murder of Ralph Stafford, received amongst other choice properties, Monmouth Castle.

Henry was shattered. It had not occurred to him that his cousin would break his promise and he had made no contingency plans for such an event. Suddenly he was a ruined man with nothing to look forward to and no prospects for his four young sons. With nothing to lose now, Henry had no need to stay in exile and he immediately started to plan his return to England to reclaim his birthright.

At his Paris quarters he was joined by another who had reason to bear King Richard a grudge, the ex-archbishop of Canterbury, Thomas Arundel, who had supported the Lords Appellant and the Merciless Parliament, and later suffered Richard's wrath. It was his brother, the Earl of Arundel, who had been so ruthlessly put to the axe on Tower Hill two years before. The Earl's teenage son, another Thomas Arundel, also found his way to Henry's side.

Henry quickly collected together a few boats and supporters. He promised them that his purpose was merely to reclaim his inheritance and that he had no intention of taking his cousin's crown. It was necessary for him to make this point, for many who backed his right to fight for his lands would not have been prepared to help him usurp the throne.

As Richard loaded his ships with almost everyone of rank, authority or fighting skill and sailed them away to Ireland, Henry brought his tiny flotilla across the Channel to England. His unlikely invasion force sailed along the Strait of Dover and then up round the east coast to land at Ravenspur a port on the mouth of the Humber long since lost to coastal erosion. Immediately men faithful to the memory of Henry's father and indignant at Richard's theft of the Lancastrian estates came to swell his invasion force. Just as immediately the weather, that had been so kind to Henry while he was at sea, turned foul and closed the ports. So, while Henry travelled round to various Lancastrian castles in

Yorkshire whipping up support, Richard wined, dined and hung around in Ireland while his soldiers tried unsuccessfully to locate and subdue the rebels.

Richard had appointed as Regent in England his only surviving uncle, Edmund Duke of York, and it was a week after Henry's landing before the weather settled enough for York to dispatch a ship to Ireland with news. Tardily, for he had not at first realised the support that Henry would muster, the Regent began to recruit an army to defend the nation. To his confusion and dismay, York found that very few lords were willing to rally to the royal standard - though one who did so was Henry's half brother John Beaufort. This lack of support was due in part to the fact that the nobles were gravely concerned with the way the King had annexed the Lancastrian estates. If it could happen to the son of John of Gaunt, then nobody's property was safe. Henry had also issued letters explaining that his return to England was because the King intended to continue with his despotic schemes and punitive taxation methods.

As the Duke of York was unable to obtain support in the south he decided to make for the west coast where he could meet up with Richard's army when it arrived back from Ireland. Henry was kept well informed of the Regent's plans by his half brother, Beaufort, and on learning of York's move towards Gloucestershire, he marched his troops down across England to intercept them. Uncle and nephew met at Berkeley Castle, between Bristol and Gloucester. York, who had had the Regency thrust upon him because the King could trust no-one else to do the job, was out of his depth. Faced with his brother's disinherited and charismatic son he simply swapped sides.

When the King sailed into Milford Haven and found no support, he fled to Conway Castle, only to find that the expected Earl of Salisbury's army had drifted away through sheer lack of enthusiasm for the cause. With knowledge of the King's moves possibly provided by York's son, the Duke of Aumale who was with Richard, Henry immediately marched his army north and established himself at Shrewsbury Castle. Here he waited while Thomas Arundel and another important ally, Henry Percy, Earl of Northumberland, journeyed to Conway to establish a basis for discussion. They explained to the King that all Henry wanted was the reinstatement of the Lancastrian lands and invited him to accompany them to Flint Castle where the two cousins could discuss terms.

Richard was relieved that Henry's demands were so reasonable; after all, he had done his best to completely ruin the man, so with just a hand-full of courtiers he set off for Flint Castle. The party had travelled only a few miles when Northumberland's troops ambushed them. The King completed his journey to Flint as a prisoner.

Henry's task now was to get his cousin to London. Knowing that there would be rescue attempts, the King's captors were forced to disguise him, and so Richard made the journey south dressed as a lowly friar, mounted on a humble pony. Perhaps, though, Henry allowed malevolence to colour his decision when he had the Earl of Salisbury travel alongside the King similarly clad and riding an equally unsplendid hack - for this was the man who, just six months before, had snubbed Henry in Paris and cost him a royal bride.

It was an uncomfortable twelve days journey for Richard, made worse by the defection of his dog, a greyhound called Math. This fickle mutt, perhaps sniffing despair, loped off and attached himself to Henry who welcomed the unworthy creature as a good omen. Just outside London the city fathers, fired with bravado now that Henry had achieved this much, were waiting to take charge of Richard. He was lodged in the Tower pending a parliamentary investigation into the legality of his actions during his twenty-two years kingship.

Henry rode directly to St Paul's to visit his father's tomb. Eyewitness accounts say that he wept - as well he might, knowing that his father would never, never have agreed to what he had done.... even less what he intended to do next. For, though Henry may not have known exactly what he was going to do when he left Paris, there is no doubt that by the time he handed his cousin over to the city fathers, he knew that he was going to take the crown.

The next step was how to do it. He favoured the idea of convincing the people that he was claiming the kingdom because it was rightfully his. To this end, he resurrected a story that his family had nursed for generations, suggesting that his great-great grandfather Prince Edmund (Crouchback) was Henry III's eldest son who had been passed over in favour of his younger brother, because of a deformity. A commission was hurriedly set up to prove this point, but the learned men, who rooted through ancient manuscripts for several weeks, came up with no evidence to support the story.

Henry had to find another route to the crown. It was decided that Richard must abdicate. Quite how the King was persuaded or, more possibly, forced to relinquish his throne is not recorded but on 29th September 1399 he signed the abdication papers. According to the official version of events, after signing away his crown, Richard took off his gold signet ring and placed it on Henry's finger, indicating that he was nominating his cousin as his successor in place of Roger Mortimer's young son.

The following day, a great assembly of Lords spiritual and temporal, shire knights and commoners gathered in front of an empty throne in Westminster Hall. It was announced that the King had abdicated, and then, just to assure the assembly that this abdication was in everybody's best interest, a long list of their ex-king's deficiencies and short-comings were read out.

Amongst this multiplicity of wrongs, perjuries, overspending and weakness of rule, Henry's own grievances were given a thorough airing, especially the confiscation of his inheritance and the murder of his uncle, Gloucester.

Once the business of the abdication was formally dealt with, it was time to deal with naming the King's successor. Thomas Arundel, Henry's constant companion through the last few turbulent months, came forward. In his newly re-appointed capacity as Archbishop of Canterbury he led his ally to the empty throne. Henry took his cue and after promising the assembly that he would right the wrongs of the previous reign, he raised his hand to show that he was wearing Richard's ring - a symbol of the fact that the abdicating King had chosen him as his successor.

And so a little boy who spent his happy childhood years at Tutbury Castle became Henry IV of England. Although the Lancastrian dynasty floundered when Henry's inadequate grandson failed to keep a grip on his magnates, Tutbury Castle, as part of the Duchy of Lancaster, remains a royal possession to this day.

Stafford Castle in the 1950s

Part 2
Stafford Castle

The Princes as portrayed by Millais.

Chapter 4
A Man With a Chip on his Shoulder:
Henry Stafford, 2nd Duke of Buckingham

At the time of the Conquest, Edwin, Earl of Mercia retained his lands under William until he rebelled and was killed in 1071. His landholdings were then split up and doled out to the Conqueror's friends and supporters in the same way that most of England had already been treated. William gave a huge tract of the Mercian estates west of Stafford to Robert, the son of his hereditary standard bearer, Sir Roger de Toeni. Robert adopted the name Stafford and built the first wooden castle on the site. This fortress, as well as being his family home and administrative quarters for his estates, served as a safe haven for his Norman retainers in times of unrest.

> Snippet The castle in Stafford mentioned as being 'recently destroyed' in the Domesday book was nothing to do with the de Toenis and was on a different site altogether.

Robert did not enjoy the Conqueror's favour in the same way as his neighbour Henry Ferrers at Tutbury Castle because the de Toeni family had been involved in a rebellion against William in Normandy before the Conquest. As a safeguard his manors had been spread across England, making the family's chance of amassing powerful allies and wealth more difficult. The ploy worked and the de Toeni-cum-Staffords wealth remained modest and they, probably on that account, remained loyal to their benefactors for generations after the Ferrers' dynasty had toppled.

In actual fact, the male line of the de Toeni-cum-Staffords ran out of steam before the end of the 12th century when the fourth Robert Stafford died without an heir. His estates devolved on his sister Millicent, who married Hervey Bagot, a local squire whose Saxon ancestors had somehow managed to hang on to their lands. When, in 1194, Hervey married Millicent, he adopted the Stafford name and saved the dynasty from extinction.

Some four hundred years later, in 1590, Edward, Lord Stafford, eschewed this Bagot connection in a letter to Hervey's descendant Richard Bagot. Richard claimed that Lord Stafford should more rightly be dubbed 'Lord Bagot' on account of the Millicent Stafford/Hervey Bagot union. By this time, the Staffords had risen way above the rest of the Bagot clan and Lord Stafford was not keen to have his family name denigrated by association with mere gentry. He wrote to Richard assuring him that he knew very well who his ancestors were and that nowhere in his pedigree did the name Bagot occur. Furthermore, he assured Richard that *'I will not exchange my name of Stafford for the name of a bag of oats, for that is your name, 'Bag Ote.'"*

> Snippet The main branch of the Bagots managed to navigate the medieval period virtually unscathed. They arrived in the 20th century with their ancestral home, Blithfield Hall near Rugeley, intact and playing host to a legendary herd of rather unfriendly creatures known locally as 'the Bagot goats'.

It was at the outbreak of the Hundred Years War, in the reign of Edward III that the House of Stafford came to prominence. Ralph Stafford, the great-great-great-great-

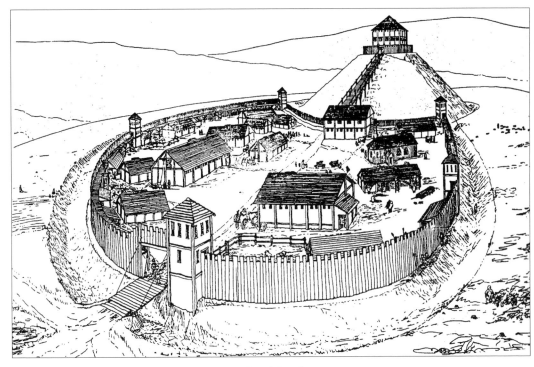

Stafford Castle.

A conjectural reconstruction of the timber phase of Stafford Castle built during the reign of William II (Rufus). *Drawings by Peter Scholefield, by permission of Stafford Borough Council.*

grandson of Millicent and Hervey, acquired his inheritance in 1308. He was a fine soldier and had already spent years fighting the Scots by the time Edward proclaimed himself King of France and took his armies across the Channel in a futile attempt to make good the claim. During 1342 Ralph led reinforcement troops to Brittany and was captured along with another nobleman Sir Henry Leon, when the town of Vannes was besieged. The King arranged an exchange between Ralph and a French noble. Sir Henry Leon, who obviously was not considered so useful, languished as a prisoner of the French for six years.

Later, when Edward III introduced his Order of the Garter, he selected 26 founder members. Ralph was amongst this elite. Then, in 1351 came the big 'thank you' for his years of loyal service - he was created Earl of Stafford. Although the earldom came with an annuity of 1,000 marks this was hardly sufficient to support such an honour - but it is unlikely that the King would have bestowed the title on his friend, had not Ralph already manoeuvred himself into a prosperous position.

He had been widowed in his thirties, and fortunately for him Edward III had not yet founded the Order of the Garter, because Ralph's wooing of his second wife, Margaret de Clare, hardly smacks of chivalry. Young Margaret's mother, a grandchild of Edward I, had inherited part of the estates of Gilbert de Clare, Earl of Gloucester. She had married Hugh de Audley and their only child, a girl, was exceedingly marriageable.

> Snippet   Margaret de Clare who inherited a third of the de Clare estates was a niece of Edward II. She was the royal bride Edward gave to his favourite, Piers Gaveston. Her daughter Margaret who married Ralph Stafford was the progeny of her second marriage.

Ralph, having covered himself with glory during his campaigns and his ambassadorial duties for the King, obviously felt that he deserved a well connected, well moneyed second wife with a tinge of royal blood about her. The eighteen years old Margaret de Clare eminently filled the bill. Ralph turned up at her home with an armed posse, kidnapped her, ravished her and then married her.

Hugh de Audley's outrage was eventually smoothed sufficiently to accept the situation and he settled his wife's share of the de Clare inheritance on Ralph and his heirs. Ralph Stafford was now affluent, titled and well connected, and could marry his children into the very top echelons of the aristocracy. In 1348 his eldest son, also Ralph, was married whilst still a child to Matilda of Lancaster (great, great grandchild of Henry III) though he died before the marriage could be consummated. Had he lived, Ralph junior would have become brother-in-law to John of Gaunt who married Matilda's sister Blanche.

Ralph and Margaret's second son, Hugh, became the 2nd Earl of Stafford in 1372 when his old war-horse of a father died. Hugh had also been kitted out with an illustrious bride. Philippa Beauchamp was daughter of Thomas, Earl of Warwick - one of the five Lords Appellant who tried to force their ideas on Richard II.

Hugh's eldest son, another Ralph, met a tragic, early death. He had grown up as one of the boy companions of Richard II. He was riding with his father to Newcastle where troops were mustering ready for an invasion of Scotland when, near York, a dispute broke out between retainers of Thomas Holland (Richard II's half brother) and Hugh Stafford's men. One of Holland's party was killed and in retaliation, Holland rode out to meet the Staffords, picked a quarrel with Ralph and slew him. Richard II swore that the death of his childhood

Ralph, Lord Stafford, depicted
on the brass of Sir Hugh
Hastings.

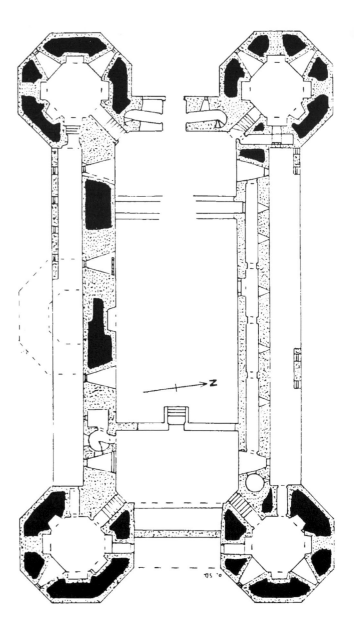

Plan of Stafford Castle.

This illustration is taken from *The Castles and
Moated Mansions of Staffordshire & the West
Midlands County* by Mike Salter.

friend should be properly avenged even though the murderer was his own kinsman, but Thomas Holland quickly married John of Gaunt's daughter Elizabeth and joined the Duke's expedition to Castile, which seemed to forestall any recrimination. Hugh Stafford, disenchanted with this crass lack of justice, went on a pilgrimage to Jerusalem and died.

Thus Hugh's second son, Thomas, became the 3rd Earl and continued the custom of top-drawer unions by marrying Anne Plantagenet, daughter of the Duke of Gloucester (Thomas of Woodstock), the youngest son of Edward III. Anne was seven at the time and before she was old enough to take on her marital responsibilities Thomas had died. His younger brother, fourteen year old William, now became the 4th Earl of Stafford and when he also died three years later, the next brother in line, Edmund, inherited not only the earldom, but in due course, his brother Thomas's royal widow.

Anne was fifteen by this time, old enough to take on the duty of providing her husband with heirs. Financially speaking, she turned out to be a better catch than Edmund could ever have dreamed of because in 1397 her father fell victim to Richard II's spleen and was murdered. During the next three years her mother Eleanor de Bohun, her only brother and her three sisters also died. This plethora of untimely deaths meant that Anne inherited from her father a claim to the Earldom of Buckingham (a title bestowed on him at Richard II's coronation) and her mother's share of the de Bohun inheritance, fabulous landed wealth. Edmund at twenty-three years of age found himself espoused to possibly the richest woman in the kingdom and his position in the social hierarchy advanced accordingly.

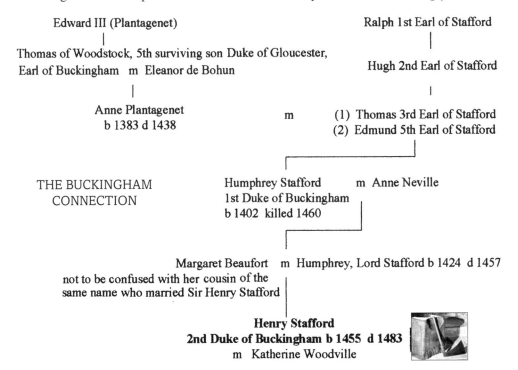

Edward III (Plantagenet)

Thomas of Woodstock, 5th surviving son Duke of Gloucester,
Earl of Buckingham m Eleanor de Bohun

Anne Plantagenet
b 1383 d 1438

m

Ralph 1st Earl of Stafford

Hugh 2nd Earl of Stafford

(1) Thomas 3rd Earl of Stafford
(2) Edmund 5th Earl of Stafford

THE BUCKINGHAM
CONNECTION

Humphrey Stafford   m Anne Neville
1st Duke of Buckingham
b 1402 killed 1460

Margaret Beaufort   m Humphrey, Lord Stafford b 1424 d 1457
not to be confused with her cousin of the
same name who married Sir Henry Stafford

Henry Stafford
2nd Duke of Buckingham b 1455 d 1483
m Katherine Woodville

During this time Henry (Bolingbroke) of Lancaster had usurped the throne and Richard II had been murdered. This left an aftermath of civil war and the descendants of William the Conqueror's Norman settlers were once again called upon to take sides.

Whereas Edmund's grandfather, the old war-horse Ralph Stafford, would, in the same circumstances, have been able to consider his options and choose whether to throw his weight behind Richard II's supporters or Henry of Lancaster, Edmund had no such choice. He owed his lofty aristocratic status to his wife's family and his murdered father-in-law was a victim of Richard's tyranny, so Edmund sided wih Lancaster.

He paid dearly for this enforced choice. The Percys, an old noble family whose chief the Duke of Northumberland had been a major force in placing Henry IV on the throne, planned a revolt. In the summer of 1403, Edmund Stafford fought against Northumberland's son, 'Harry Hotspur', at the Battle of Shrewsbury - and lost his life. He was twenty-six years old and his heir, Humphrey was still a baby. Humphrey was too young to know of Henry IV's troubled reign and pain-wracked death. And when Henry V cranked up England's claim to the throne of France in 1415, Humphrey was still too young to fight at Agincourt.

He married Anne Neville, grand-daughter of John of Gaunt and Katherine Swynford. This marriage strengthened his royal connections and his dedication to the Lancastrian monarchy. By the time he was twenty two he was admitted to the royal council and during the long years of Henry VI's minority, he was very much involved in affairs of state.

Although Humphrey inherited the Earldom of Stafford from his father, it was not until his mother's death that he became the Earl of Buckingham and inherited fifty percent of the de Bohun inheritance. He was in his mid-thirties by this time and his mother's assets secured his position amongst the wealthiest in the land. It meant that when Henry VI wanted to show his appreciation of Humphrey's long years of loyalty and support, the Earl was in a position to support a dukedom, and the King created him Duke of Buckingham.

Humphrey's wife provided him with six sons and three daughters. Most of these children grew to maturity and their father saw that they were married into the leading families of the era. In fact, Charles VII of France flirted with the idea of marrying the Dauphin to one of Buckingham's daughters and although the negotiations fizzled out, it shows how well Duke Humphrey was esteemed. The Duke was fifty three years old in 1455 when the Yorkists' seething discontent at Lancastrian rule erupted and the Wars of the Roses began in earnest. The first battle took place at St Albans and Humphrey was commander-in-chief of the royal armies. The skirmish was over very quickly, but the Lancastrians lost the day and Humphrey as commander was seen to be responsible for the heavy losses amongst their senior officers. More painfully, his eldest son, Humphrey Lord Stafford, received wounds which later killed him.

Humphrey lived a full fifty-eight years and knew his fair share of glory and heartache. He helped politically, financially and emotionally to support the hen-pecked and weak-witted Henry VI. In 1439 he travelled to Calais as an ambassador seeking, unsuccessfully, an end to the Hundred Years War. He also officiated at the trial of Joan of Arc. During one of King Henry's periods of insanity the Queen bore their only child and it was Humphrey who took the baby boy in his arms to the inert King, beseeching him to recognise the infant as heir to the throne.

Snippet Henry VI lapsed into deep 'melancholia' in 1452 and was still unable to talk or recognise people when Prince Edward was born in 1453. It was some months before he was 'compos mentis' enough to acknowledge he had fathered a son. Popular rumour suggested that his Queen had made a cuckold of him.

Like his father and his elder son, Humphrey paid a high price for his loyalty to the Lancastrian dream when he was killed in 1460 at the Battle of Northampton commanding the royalist troops against the Yorkists. Humphrey's grandson Henry, aged five, became the 2nd Duke of Buckingham and the Crown eagerly took up its lucrative rights of wardship.

Now, before I go into what happened next, we need some genealogy. You may find the following paragraphs simply repetitive but bear with me because it is very important.

William the Conqueror's Norman forbears had adopted the French language and the French Salic law. In Normandy Salic Law dictated that a female could not inherit the crown or pass on a title to it, but in England this was never officially adopted.

333 years after the Conquest, John of Gaunt's son took the throne from Richard II in 1399. Even if Richard deserved to lose the crown on account of his tyranny, Henry Bolingbroke's claim to be next in line was not clear cut. His father John of Gaunt, was the third of Edward III's sons to grow to maturity and have children. The eldest son was Richard II's father, Prince Edward, the Black Prince, next was Lionel and then there was John. Lionel had a daughter Philippa who married Edmund Mortimer, 3rd Earl of March. They had a son Roger whom Richard II, being childless, nominated as heir presumptive. Roger was killed when he was only 25 years old, but by then he had fathered five children. The eldest of this brood was Anne and her progeny were destined to star as major protagonists during the deadly quarrels for the crown, the Wars of the Roses.

If you ask half a dozen different historians what caused these wars you will get half a dozen different answers and somewhere amongst them there would be the theory that too

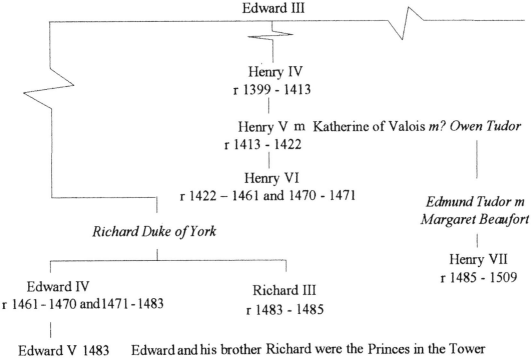

Edward III

Henry IV
r 1399 - 1413

Henry V m Katherine of Valois *m? Owen Tudor*
r 1413 - 1422

Henry VI
r 1422 – 1461 and 1470 - 1471

Edmund Tudor m
Margaret Beaufort

Richard Duke of York

Henry VII
r 1485 - 1509

Edward IV
r 1461 - 1470 and 1471 - 1483

Richard III
r 1483 - 1485

Edward V 1483   Edward and his brother Richard were the Princes in the Tower

THE KINGS THROUGHOUT PART TWO

THE STAFFORD-BEAUFORT CONNECTION

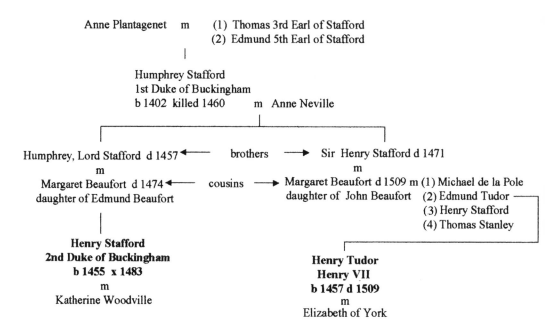

Anne Plantagenet   m   (1) Thomas 3rd Earl of Stafford
                           (2) Edmund 5th Earl of Stafford

Humphrey Stafford
1st Duke of Buckingham
b 1402 killed 1460   m Anne Neville

Humphrey, Lord Stafford d 1457 ◄—— brothers ——► Sir Henry Stafford d 1471
                m   m
Margaret Beaufort d 1474 ◄—— cousins ——► Margaret Beaufort d 1509 m (1) Michael de la Pole
daughter of Edmund Beaufort   daughter of John Beaufort   (2) Edmund Tudor ——
                                                                            (3) Henry Stafford
                                                                            (4) Thomas Stanley

Henry Stafford
2nd Duke of Buckingham
b 1455 x 1483
                m   **Henry Tudor**
Katherine Woodville   **Henry VII**
                                               b 1457 d 1509
                                                    m
                                               Elizabeth of York

THE YORKIST CONNECTION

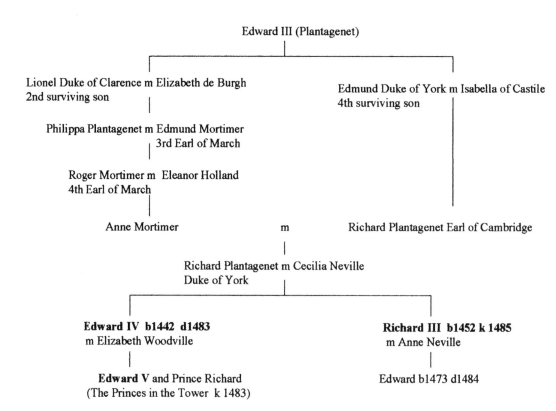

Edward III (Plantagenet)

Lionel Duke of Clarence m Elizabeth de Burgh   Edmund Duke of York m Isabella of Castile
2nd surviving son   4th surviving son

Philippa Plantagenet m Edmund Mortimer
                    3rd Earl of March

Roger Mortimer m Eleanor Holland
4th Earl of March

Anne Mortimer   m   Richard Plantagenet Earl of Cambridge

Richard Plantagenet m Cecilia Neville
Duke of York

Edward IV b1442 d1483   **Richard III b1452 k 1485**
m Elizabeth Woodville   m Anne Neville

Edward V and Prince Richard   Edward b1473 d1484
(The Princes in the Tower k 1483)

many of Edward III's sons survived to manhood. Five out of eight male offspring grew up to marry and proliferate and the lack of a law of succession gave the descendants of these princes an excuse to cast an acquisitive eye on the crown.

Edward III's fourth surviving son was Edmund of Langley, Duke of York. He married Isabella, Don Pedro of Castile's youngest daughter. Their son Richard married Anne the daughter of Roger Mortimer. So Richard and Anne were both descendants of Edward III, and both had a claim to the throne. Their son, Richard, Duke of York, would father the future Edward IV and Richard III.

Snippet It was Richard, Duke of York, (great-great grandchild of Edward III's second son, Lionel) who first officially adopted the name Plantagenet though it had been in use by the Anjou/Plantagenet dynasty since Matilda married Geoffrey Count of Anjou's son in the 12th century. Richard did this to emphasise that his lineage gave him a stronger claim to the throne than the usurping Lancastrian dynasty.

The fifth son of Edward III was Thomas of Woodstock, who was created Earl of Buckingham and later Duke of Gloucester by his nephew Richard II. His daughter, Anne Plantagenet, married Edmund, 5th Earl of Stafford. Their son Humphrey Stafford became the 1st Duke of Buckingham and died at the Battle of Northampton in 1460 when the House of Lancaster was overthrown and the ineffectual Henry VI deposed. Humphrey's grandson, Henry Stafford, was about five years old at the time and became the 2nd Duke of Buckingham.

So back to the story. Edward IV, the first Yorkist king, was 19 years old and unmarried when he snatched the throne in 1461. His advisors spent time planning a grand marriage alliance for him within the French royal family, but just at the final negotiations, Edward informed them that he had secretly married a widow, Elizabeth Woodville.

Elizabeth Woodville's ancestors were minor gentry, although while Elizabeth was a girl, Henry VI had created her father Baron Rivers. No king of England since the Conquest had married a commoner and the fact that Edward had married for love did not impress his hard-bitten councillors - his duty was to form an alliance. Her lack of pedigree was not the Council's only concern; her first husband Sir John Grey had been killed fighting against the Yorkists. Her father and elder brother had also fought with the Lancastrians and only swapped their allegiance to Edward when it seemed the most expedient thing to do. Elizabeth herself had served as a maid-of-honour at the Lancastrian court of Henry VI.

All this made Elizabeth unpopular with her husband's kinsmen and councillors right from the start. A more sensitive woman might have worked to make herself acceptable, but the Queen brought her family to court where they greedily sought royal patronage. And what a family it was. Father, brothers, sisters (she was the eldest of sixteen) and her two sons by her first husband, all enjoyed the royal bounty by way of titled estates or influential marriages.

It was in the pursuit of a suitably wealthy and well-connected husband for one of her younger sisters that Henry Stafford fell victim to Elizabeth Woodville's scheming. Edward IV had purchased young Henry Stafford's wardship from the Duke of Buckingham's executors and the young boy was placed in the Queen's household. Elizabeth and her family were, of course, committed Yorkists by this time, but growing up in such an

Elizabeth Woodville.

environment did not stop Henry from having an awareness of his Lancastrian roots. He would know that his father and his grandfather had lost their lives fighting against the very people who now cared for him. His disdain for the Woodvilles, however, did not save him from marriage when he was eleven years old to the Queen's eight year old sister Katherine.

Probably because of the scorn he showed for his Woodville wife and the rest of her clan, Henry did not prosper at Edward's court. As a fabulously wealthy Duke and brother-in-law of the King, he could have expected high political appointments but Edward kept him at a distance. The King would of course have been well aware that this young Lancastrian was as much a descendant of Edward III as he was himself.

Being forced into an 'inferior' marriage and being snubbed politically, were only two of the grudges Henry held against Edward. There was also the matter of the de Bohun inheritance. Through his great-great-grandmother Eleanor he had inherited half of the de Bohun wealth, the other half had devolved to Eleanor's sister Mary, wife of Henry IV. This had passed to her son Henry V and in turn to her grandson Henry VI. When Edward IV seized the crown he claimed it along with the rest of the deposed King's assets.

Henry felt that the King had no right to this. He reasoned that as Henry VI had died with no heir, the De Bohun inheritance should track back three generations to when it was originally split between the two sisters and revert to him. Edward was not listening. These grievances gave Henry a focus for his ill will and made him a dissident waiting for a cause. And when, in April 1483, Edward IV died unexpectedly, there were plenty of causes: that of Richard, Duke of Gloucester, the dead King's only surviving brother and a man suspicious of the Queen and her clan; that of the family of another brother, the Duke of Clarence, whom Elizabeth had persuaded the King to execute as a traitor; and that of William, Lord Hastings, a friend of Edward for many years who enjoyed high office. Hastings and the King indulged their penchant for wenching together, so, of course, Queen Elizabeth was not enamoured of him.

Snippet   George Duke of Clarence is the fellow who was famously drowned in a butt of Malmsey in the Tower. His mother (who was also Edward IV's mother) beseeched Edward not to allow his brother to suffer the horrors of a traitor's death and so this unique form of execution was devised. Any rights of succession to the throne of George's heir were automatically forfeit when his father was condemned as a traitor.

And then there were the Woodvilles.... Edward IV's eldest son was twelve years old when his father died. He had been created Prince of Wales soon after his birth and provided with his own establishment at Ludlow Castle on the Welsh borders. A Council of the Welsh Marches was established and the Queen's brother Anthony Woodville, Earl Rivers, as Governor of the Council was given the responsibility of rearing the Prince. Other Woodville kinsmen, Sir Richard Haute and Sir Richard Grey, the Prince's half brother, were also closely involved in this and lived with him at Ludlow Castle. This surfeit of his mother's relatives meant that Prince Edward grew up totally submerged in Woodville influences.

Although Edward IV had turned a blind eye to the animosity caused by the rise of the Woodvilles, he was well aware that it existed and when he realised he was dying he tried, for his son's sake, to cull their power. He added a codicil to his will that his brother Richard, Duke of Gloucester, was to be Protector of the Realm during the young King's minority. Earl Rivers was to be relieved of his appointment as Governor and the Queen, who had originally been named as an executor of her husband's will, was given no powers at all.

The Woodvilles immediately set to scheming a way round the King's amended will. They had been used to power during Edward's reign and now, with their twelve year old scion on the throne, they would be omnipotent, providing they could keep Richard of Gloucester at bay. They knew that his appointment as Protector would cease as soon as the new King was crowned when a Council would take over the government of the country, so they arranged for the coronation to take place early the following month. In the meantime they sent news of the King's death to Earl Rivers at Ludlow Castle and instructed him to bring his nephew to London ready to be crowned. They did not bother to inform Gloucester that his brother had died.

When Lord Hastings realised that the Duke of Gloucester had not been told of Edward's death he was horrified. It did not augur well for the late King's wishes. Hastings' loyalty meant that he could not allow the Woodvilles to set a date for the coronation without Gloucester being aware of what was going on. He wrote to the Duke suggesting to him that if he wanted his brother's wishes upheld, it would be necessary to break the Woodvilles' stranglehold at court. The best way of doing that, the letter advised, was to take physical control of the new King. Hastings of course, was well aware of Henry Stafford's loathing of the Woodvilles and so he wrote to him too, telling him exactly what he had suggested to Gloucester.

Henry was at Brecon on the Welsh Marches when he received the letter and he realised that if the Duke of Gloucester was to fulfil Edward IV's wishes, he would have to come to London - putting himself into Woodville territory where he would be at risk from the young King's clan. They would surely find a way to stop Gloucester taking up the protectorate and getting his knees under the Council table.

So, Henry wrote to Gloucester, offering him men and support. What were his motives? Perhaps nothing more than spite - the desire to help bring down the family who had, in his opinion, denigrated him. There was also the de Bohun inheritance - obviously the Woodvilles would not allow these huge estates to pass out of the royal possession while they had control of the young Edward V. But if he gave his assistance to Gloucester at this crucial point, then Gloucester would surely be generous to him once the Woodvilles' power had been negated. Or, was there a more obscure and sinister motive?

There must have been a frantic toing and froing of messengers between the Duke of Gloucester and Henry as they plotted to capture the young King making his way south towards London in the care of his uncle, Earl Rivers, and an escort of 2,000 men. Also in the King's retinue was Sir Richard Haute, his tutor Bishop Alcock and his well-beloved chamberlain Sir Thomas Vaughan, the man who had more or less taken on the role of a mother figure in the Ludlow establishment.

Gloucester sent notification to Rivers that he and Henry intended to meet the royal escort in Northampton and accompany young Edward to London. This would all have seemed reasonable enough to the Earl - it was no bad thing to have the King's uncle of Gloucester and the Grand Duke of Buckingham as travelling companions when he made his entry into the City, it would project a fine display of family loyalty and pageantry.

However shortly after Edward's party arrived at Northampton, where they intended to wait for the two dukes to join them as arranged, the King's half brother Sir Richard Grey (who was Earl River's nephew) arrived from London. The Woodville dominated Council was wary of Gloucester's intentions and Grey's race across country was to tell Rivers to get the King to London with all urgency so that nothing could stop the coronation five days later on May 4th.

Without waiting for Gloucester and Buckingham, Rivers moved the royal party on to Stony Stratford, just fifty miles outside London. After seeing the King comfortably lodged, the earl and his nephew set off again for Northampton to greet the dukes and give them some feeble excuse about insufficient accommodation.

Gloucester and Henry had already arrived in Northampton and had time to assimilate the Woodvilles' incredible snub. They had also had time to decide how to play their hand and when Rivers and Grey turned up, the two dukes greeted them without any show of pique. The four men enjoyed a leisurely dinner together and when the Woodville contingent eventually left for their lodgings at an inn further along the High Street, they must have felt huge relief that the evening had gone off so amicably. But while these two men indulged the sleep of the relaxed and well-imbibed, Gloucester and Henry discussed their plans. The next morning Rivers and Grey awoke to find themselves prisoners within their lodgings. When the two dukes turned up they announced that Earl Rivers was under arrest for attempting to keep the King away from his paternal uncle, the man appointed by Edward IV to be his Protector.

The Dukes then set off with their escort parties and Sir Richard Grey to catch up with the royal convoy. The boy King was greeted with due ceremony and then told that his uncle Rivers had been arrested and that his travelling companions were to be removed. He was told that his Woodville relations were plotting the death of the very man his father had thought best to advise and care for him during his youth - his uncle Gloucester.

> Snippet   No proof has ever been found that Rivers, Grey or any of the young King's travelling companions had plotted to murder Richard, Duke of Gloucester. It is likely that Gloucester and Henry invented this story to discredit the King's Woodville kin.

The twelve year old boy was distraught. These men had been his constant companions at Ludlow castle, his trusty servants, his friends, his kin. How could his uncle of Gloucester, a near stranger to him, accuse them of plotting murder. Needless to say, the poor little fellow cried as Vaughan, Haute and Grey were arrested and taken away. The rest of the King's escort were dismissed and then Edward was taken back to Northampton in the company of the two dukes.

When the dowager Queen Elizabeth learned of the coup she knew that the tables had been turned. With Gloucester in power, the Woodvilles were in danger. She immediately fled with her younger son Prince Richard, her five daughters and a few more of her near relatives, into the sanctuary at Westminster Abbey.

On 3rd May, Edward V restarted his journey to London, this time escorted by his uncle Gloucester and Duke Henry. Although due pomp and ceremony was observed throughout the journey, the King had been kidnapped and his eventual lodgings in the Tower of London were in fact a prison. Within days, the Council confirmed Gloucester in his role as Lord Protector and a new date in late June was set for the coronation. Until Edward V was actually crowned, the Protector was King in all but name and Gloucester immediately used his new powers to reward his ally's support. The honours that had failed to come Henry Stafford's way during the previous reign were now heaped on him. He was created Constable of England, Chief Justice, Lord Chamberlain of Wales and he replaced Rivers on the Council of the Marches where he was already a huge land holder. There were promises too that Gloucester's only son should marry one of Henry's daughters. And very importantly, steps were made towards transferring the disputed de Bohun inheritance to him.

Henry Stafford, 2nd Duke of Buckingham had achieved what he wanted, acclaim and recognition, the fall of the Woodvilles, and the de Bohun inheritance. What more could he want? The two dukes were acutely aware that once the King was crowned and the Protectorate ended, Gloucester would have to step down and take his place on the Regency Council, set up to rule during Edward's minority. But the King would be fourteen in less than two years and he would then bring back into the political arena his mother and the rest of the Woodville clan. The Woodvilles would demand vengeance. Gloucester and Henry could not allow this to happen and there was only one way to stop it!

Troops from Gloucester's and Henry's northern territories were ordered to make their way to London while plans to neutralise the King's family, friends and supporters were put into operation. Lord Hastings, the man who had first alerted the two dukes to the Woodvilles' intentions, had outlived his usefulness. He was immensely wealthy and influential on the Council and his determination to see his old friend's son succeed to his father's throne would henceforth render him a hindrance. Hastings had voiced his concerns amongst members of the Council that he believed Gloucester intended to oust the boy King. The Duke chose to interpret this as treason and turned up with an armed escort at a Council meeting where he denounced Hastings along with certain colleagues, including Bishop Morton and Thomas, Lord Stanley. The Bishop and Stanley were arrested while Hastings was handed over to Duke Henry for execution. Although Hastings pleaded his innocence and the right to a trial, he was dragged away to Tower Green and within a few hours of his arrest, was beheaded on a makeshift dais.

Instructions for the execution of the King's original companions on his journey, Vaughan, Haute, the dowager Queen's son Richard Grey and her brother Anthony Woodville, Earl Rivers, were sent out to the northern strongholds where these man were held prisoners. Before news of the imminent executions had filtered through to Elizabeth in her Westminster sanctuary, Gloucester had 'persuaded' her to part with her younger son Richard, Duke of York. This had been no easy feat because Elizabeth was terrified - terrified for her own life, terrified for her daughters' lives and most of all terrified for the life of her nine year old son who, in the event of anything happening to his brother, would become King.

It took a show of armed strength outside the sanctuary and a promise of the boy's safe return after the coronation before she released young Richard. The prince was taken by Gloucester's envoy to the Palace of Westminster where he was greeted with due deference by Duke Henry and then fleetingly taken to meet his uncle the Protector. Afterwards, the little fellow, who was apparently overjoyed at his release from the confines of the sanctuary, continued his journey by river to the Tower to join his brother.

London was by this time filling up with all manner of redoubtable personages summoned for the coronation and also for the parliament scheduled to open three days after the crowning. But who was to be crowned?

Although the seizing of the boy King and the imprisonment of his escort had unsettled many of the nobles, they had still been prepared to give the Protector and his right-hand man, Henry Duke of Buckingham, the benefit of the doubt. But since the brutal execution of Hastings these men were thoroughly nervous - they all had homes, families and fortunes to protect. It was all looking very much as if their loyalties were about to be tested. They were...

Instead of the expected coronation on 22nd June the people of London were treated to a sermon. They were informed that the late Edward IV was the result of his mother's liaison with one of her husband's courtiers and that neither Edward IV nor either of his sons was legally entitled to the throne. Gloucester, on the other hand, so the bemused crowds were informed, resembled his father the late Duke of York and was, therefore, the rightful king.

This story did not go down at all well and so a couple of days later Gloucester and Henry came up with another angle. The next round of propaganda suggested that Edward had bigamously married Elizabeth Woodville after already pre-contracting to marry another paramour. If this allegation was true, Edward IV and Elizabeth Woodville had indeed lived together bigamously for nearly twenty years and their ten offspring were all bastards.

This scandalous accusation, for which no proof has ever surfaced, seemed to be more palatable to the public than the previous story, because Edward was such a notorious womaniser. Besides, the nobles were now pretty sure that Gloucester was determined to have the crown one way or another. His 'kidnapping' of the King and Prince Richard, the execution without trial of Hastings, and the imprisonment of Rivers, Grey, Vaughan and Haute were persuasive. Submission seemed to be the only safe option. When, later that month, Henry suggested to the lords that they should accept Gloucester as their king, there was no wholesale disagreement - if no wholesale approval.

Two days later Gloucester turned up in Westminster Hall, took his seat on the marble throne and began his reign as Richard III. The day before, at Pontefract Castle, Earl Rivers, Richard Grey, Haute and Vaughan were beheaded and their naked bodies buried with scant ceremony. A splendid coronation for Richard and his Queen took place in early July when Henry had a prestigious role to play as the King's train bearer. Lord Stanley, who had been restored to favour following the Hastings debacle, was instructed that he was to attend the coronation with his wife, Margaret Beaufort, who was to have the honour of carrying Queen Anne's train.

> Snippet Henry's wife, Katherine Woodville did not attend Richard III's coronation. She was, after all, a sister of the ex Queen Elizabeth who, since her marriage with Edward IV had been declared unlawful, was known simply as Elizabeth Grey. Katherine's 'low birth' had always been an embarrassment to Henry and on this occasion she simply would not do.

So far, Henry Stafford had acted as eager kingmaker for his distant kinsman, but during the coronation ceremony, just at the moment when Archbishop Bourchier placed the crown on Richard's head, it is said he looked away. Surely this was Henry's greatest moment, so why could he not bear to see Richard crowned? He had played a major part in this almost bloodless usurpation.... and it had all gone so well. So well in fact, that perhaps he could think about a re-run and put himself on the throne. After all he was just as much a direct descendant of Edward III as the new King.

There were still problems to be overcome of course. Neither Richard nor anybody else would be safe on the throne while men loyal to Edward IV's memory were refusing to accept the pre-contract story and were whispering that the crown really belonged to young Edward V. There was the Woodville faction: the ex Queen, her surviving Grey son and their allies, all would seek to reinstall the boy King on his throne. In fact, while Edward and his younger brother lived there would always be a focus for rebellion.

The murder of the Princes, and their burial under a stone staircase in the Tower, happened within a short while of Richard's coronation. Whether Henry Stafford was actively involved in ordering their death is a matter of debate, but when the King set off on his Royal progress of the Midlands and the North a fortnight after he was crowned, there is no record that Henry went with him. This in itself is hardly evidence to point a finger at Henry and he may well have remained in London because he was the only person that Richard trusted to guard his capital... in which case the King had made a grave mistake.

Richard III

Once the Princes were dead, Henry had no more need of Richard but to achieve his end he needed to bring together the Woodvilles and another who, so far in this narrative, has put in no more than a cameo appearance. Margaret Beaufort, who had carried Queen Anne's train at the coronation, was Henry's aunt. She was forty years old in 1483 and as the name Beaufort suggests, a descendant of John of Gaunt and his third wife Katherine Swynford - a great grand-daughter in fact. She was a Lancastrian by birth, by inclination and also on account of the aspirations she held for her only child, Henry Tudor.

She was married at the age of twelve to Edmund Tudor, Earl of Richmond, and produced her only child a year later. By the time the baby was born, Margaret was a widow under the protection of her brother-in-law, Jasper Tudor, Earl of Pembroke, at his castle in Pembrokeshire. Humphrey Stafford, Duke of Buckingham, had estates on the Marches and he and Jasper Tudor were drawn together as Lancastrian supporters. They decided that Duke Humphrey's second son, Sir Henry Stafford, should marry the young widow.

The couple married and lived quietly together rearing Margaret's son, Henry, at Pembroke Castle. Jasper Tudor was busy fighting for his beleaguered King, Henry VI. When in 1461, Edward IV deposed Henry VI, Jasper's castle was commandeered by the Yorkist, Sir William Herbert. Herbert found there a charming trio - Sir Henry Stafford, Margaret and the four year old Henry Tudor. Edward VI allowed Herbert to purchase the wardship of Henry Tudor and the child was taken to live at Raglan Castle. He stayed with his foster family for the next nine years while the Lancastrians and the Yorkists struggled for the throne until the decisive battle of Tewkesbury saw the Lancastrian army destroyed and Henry VI's only son slain.

Henry Tudor's descent through his mother from Edward III's son, John of Gaunt, now rendered him the Lancastrian's nearest claimant to the throne. Jasper Tudor realised that his nephew's life was seriously in danger and managed to seize him and whisk him away to the Continent where he stayed for the next twelve years - watching.... and waiting.... .

It was now, in the late summer of 1483, that Henry Stafford, 2nd Duke of Buckingham, decided to court the friendship of Henry Tudor's mother, Margaret Beaufort. By this time those loyal to the memory of Edward IV had formed themselves into an opposition. With the backing of Elizabeth Woodville they were planning to spring young Edward from the Tower and reinstate him on the throne. Uprisings were to take place simultaneously in the South, the Midlands and Wales while Richard was in the North courting his subjects.

But news that the Princes were dead leaked out and left the rebels with no focus for their rebellion. Nobody quite knows who started the rumours but it seems unimaginable that Richard would have wanted the boys murdered while he was away from the capital and unable to deal with the trouble that would follow on such ghastly news. For Henry Stafford, though, it was perfect timing because it gave him the opportunity to divert the passions of the rebels to his own ends. Duke Henry and Margaret Beaufort came up with a scheme whereby Margaret contacted her son, Henry Tudor and suggested that if he would promise to marry Edward IV's elder daughter, Elizabeth of York, he, Henry Stafford would persuade Elizabeth Woodville to back the Tudor claim to the throne and help overthrow Richard III.

Henry's persuasive charm, which had convinced his peers to accept Richard, just four months earlier, was now turned on the ex-Queen in favour of Henry Tudor. It was a lot to ask of Elizabeth Woodville. This man had been a constant source of worry to her husband throughout his reign, his very existence had been a veiled threat to his kingdom, a figurehead for Lancastrian malcontents to gather round. Duke Henry, though, persuaded Elizabeth that this route was her only chance of seeing her progeny recover the throne.

Thus it was that Elizabeth Woodville, mother of the murdered Yorkist King, united with Margaret Beaufort, mother of the Lancastrian quasi-heir, to oust Richard III and place their own offspring on the throne as joint rulers. Once the two mothers were in agreement, Duke Henry wrote to Henry Tudor in France, putting the plan to him and suggesting an invasion date of 18th October. Henry Tudor and his uncle Jasper accepted the challenge.

So far, so good. How easily it was all falling into place for Henry Stafford. Perhaps once the rebellion got under way he would use his oratory, just as he had done in June on behalf of Richard, only this time, he would persuade the people that he was their rightful king. Far from promoting the claim of Henry Tudor, he would remind them of his doubtful origins - the young man's lineage was so littered with bastardy that his claim to the throne was contemptible. On top of that, hadn't Henry IV specifically barred John of Gaunt's Beaufort clan from the line of succession.

> Snippet Henry Tudor was a great-great-grandson of Edward III, through his mother Margaret Beaufort who was a descendant of John of Gaunt and Katherine Swynford. The children of the Gaunt/Swynford liaison were legitimated by Richard II after their parent's marriage, but their half brother Henry Bolingbroke specifically banned them from the line of succession when he became King. On Tudor's paternal side there was also the slur of illegitimacy as there was no proof that his grandfather Owen Tudor was ever married to his grandmother Queen Katherine, the widow of Henry V. On the other hand, Henry Stafford Duke of Buckingham was a great-great-great grandson of Edward III and although his claim travelled through a female line - Anne Plantagenet his great-grandmother - there was certainly no illegitimacy. Well, at least, not on his father's side.

Then, just to smooth out any doubts of those who felt that Edward IV's throne belonged to his next living kin, Princess Elizabeth of York, he would have his marriage to Katherine Woodville annulled on the basis that he had been forced into it while a minor, and he would marry the princess himself. (I am giving Henry the benefit of a few finer feelings which he may not have possessed. If he had destroyed the Princes, he was unlikely to baulk at murdering a resented wife who stood between him and the crown).

There were three things that Duke Henry had not taken into account: his own lack of military finesse, the weather and, finally, the unreliability of medieval, conscript troops. From the 3rd October when Henry Tudor set sail from Brittany, the whole undertaking fell apart. His small fleet ran into a storm and he was forced to turn back to port. Although 18th October had been set for the rebellion, insurgents in Kent rose eight days early. Their intention to take London failed and the captured rebels were tortured into giving details of the conspiracy and Duke Henry's involvement. Word of his former ally's double-dealing was immediately sent to the King at Lincoln. Richard was deeply shocked and greatly disappointed at Henry's betrayal and swiftly proclaimed him a traitor. As gales devastated Wales and the West Country, the King planned his defence strategy.

On the 18th, Henry Tudor, now seriously behind schedule, again set sail from France. Meanwhile Duke Henry, who was not a soldier like his Stafford forebears, began to march his troops from Brecon, over the Welsh Border, to link up with the south-west rebels before

THE LANCASTRIAN CONNECTION

Edward III (Plantagenet)

|

John of Gaunt (Plantagenet) Duke of Lancaster   m (3) Katherine Swynford. The four children of this
3rd surviving son   union adopted the name Beaufort (children all
                                       born before the marriage)

John Beaufort m Margaret Holland

John Beaufort m Margaret Beauchamp   Edmund Beaufort m Eleanor Beauchamp

Margaret Beaufort m (1) John de la Pole - annulled   Margaret Beaufort m Humphrey Stafford
  b 1443 d 1509   (2) Edmund Tudor d 1456   b 1437 d 1474   b1424 d 1457
             (3) Henry Stafford d 1471   son of Humphrey 1st
             (4) Thomas Stanley d 1504   Duke of Buckingham

Henry VII (Henry Tudor) b1457 d 1509   **Henry Stafford 2nd Duke Buckingham**
m Elizabeth of York   **b 1455 x 1483**
                                       m Katherine Woodville

Henry VII, Henry Tudor, was the first king of the great Tudor period.
He presided over a period of learning, law-making and tolerance.

the King could amass his forces. It was mid-October and ten days of torrential rain had caused the banks of the River Severn to burst flooding the fords and sweeping away the bridges that Henry intended to cross. Under these appalling conditions, his Welsh conscripts, wet, hungry and without any passion for their leader's cause became fractious and uncooperative.

By the 24th the King had put a £1,000 reward on Duke Henry's head. He had also started marching south to intercept him. But he need not have concerned himself. Duke Henry had not the leadership qualities or the tactical know-how of his grandfather Humphrey or great-great-great grandfather Ralph, and he was unable to hold his unruly conscripts together. Within days they deserted him.

Duke Henry fled. He made his way to the Forest of Dean where he sought protection in the home of one of his tenants, Ralph Banastre. No doubt the thought of £1,000 helped Banastre to come to a speedy decision as to where his loyalties lay and he took little time in turning his fugitive lord over to the royalists. Meanwhile, Henry Tudor arrived off the coast of Wales, learned that the rebellion had been routed and turned his invasion fleet back to the Continent.

Duke Henry was taken in handcuffs to Salisbury where he was given a hurried trial and sentenced to death as a traitor. He sought desperately an interview with Richard who had arrived in the city with his army, though, under the circumstances, one wonders what Henry thought he could say that would save his neck.

Snippet   We know one of the last people to visit Edward V was Dr Argentein. The youth was depressed, hadn't been looking after himself and was probably suffering with toothache. When two small skeletons were discovered under a stone staircase in the Tower in 1674 they were presumed to be those of the two Princes. They were examined in the early 20th century and it was found that the jawbone of the larger skull was diseased. It has been proposed that the owner of this jaw (Edward V) would have been in continual pain, and perhaps unlikely to survive into adulthood. If the Duke of Gloucester was aware of his nephew's unhappy condition, Edward's younger brother Richard of York, as next in line, was an extremely important pawn.

He never had the opportunity to try because the King refused to see him and issued instructions for his execution to take place immediately - and even though it was a Sunday, Henry Stafford, 2nd Duke of Buckingham, was executed in Salisbury Market Place on 2nd November, 1483.

So, the Staffordshire barons notched up another abysmal failure. Only one success out of four so far..... but we still have two more to go.

Part 3
Dudley Castle

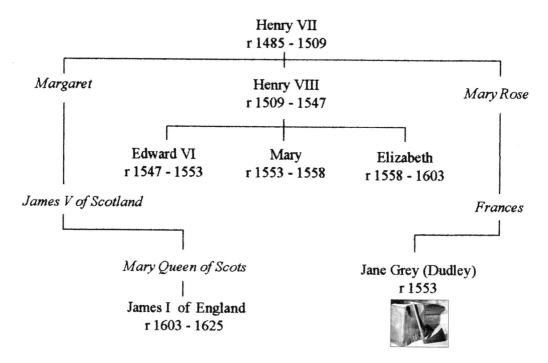

Henry VII
r 1485 - 1509

Margaret

Henry VIII
r 1509 - 1547

Mary Rose

Edward VI
r 1547 - 1553

Mary
r 1553 - 1558

Elizabeth
r 1558 - 1603

James V of Scotland

Frances

Mary Queen of Scots

James I of England
r 1603 - 1625

Jane Grey (Dudley)
r 1553

Dudley Castle taken from a tethered balloon.
Photograph courtesy of John Griffin, Friends of Dudley Castle.

Chapter 5
The Man Who Founded the Royal House of Dudley:
John Dudley, Duke of Northumberland

Unlike the de Toeni-cum-Stafford family, Ansculf of Picquigny, the first Baron of Dudley, did not establish a dynasty. There is no doubt that William the Conqueror was well pleased with the support he had received from Ansculf because he was appointed Sheriff of Buckinghamshire and given huge swathes of land in that area.

In 1066, Edwin the Saxon Earl of Mercia still retained his Midlands lands, but when he rebelled, King William put Ansculf in charge of defences in South Staffordshire, with instructions to build a castle. Earl Edwin was murdered in 1071 while escaping to Scotland to avoid the Conqueror's wrath and his lands were allocated amongst the Norman chieftains. Ansculf received a generous portion of Staffordshire, parts of Warwickshire, and in Worcestershire he was given, amongst other lands, Dudley.

So, how come Dudley Castle gets a mention in a book about Staffordshire barons and their ambitions, you ask? Well, it is true that Dudley was never in Staffordshire, not even before the massive reorganisation in 1974 when the Black Country, including Dudley, disappeared into the newly created county of the West Midlands. The castle, though, has a different story.

We do not know exactly when the original wooden castle was thrown up and we are only assuming that Ansculf did the job because his name is the first to be associated with it. We do not know who picked Dudley's hilly outcrop as the castle site. Perhaps it was William, after one of his two visits to Staffordshire to quell rebellions between 1066 and 1070, or was it Ansculf who recognised the strategic importance of Dudley's 'gateway to the south'? We do know that the castle was built in direct response to a need for fortification during the unsettled years after the Conquest, and it was built on land belonging to Earl Edwin - who did not die until 1071. William considered that the castle belonged to him and not to Earl Edwin and so he annexed Dudley's massive hill to the nearest estate that was his - Sedgley. Now the Manor of Sedgley was in Staffordshire so that is how Dudley Castle came to be in Staffordshire while Dudley itself remained in Worcestershire. Right, now that I have vindicated myself, I will get on with the story.

Ansculf's son, William Fitz Ansculf, either died without a male heir, or else rebelled and lost his castle, because in 1093 the Barony of Dudley belonged to Fulke Paganell. Fulke may have come into the Dudley lands through marriage, of course - if he married Ansculf's daughter for instance, though there is no record of a daughter. If Fitz Ansculf joined a rebellion against William II then his lands may have been confiscated and reallocated to Fulke Paganell - as happened to Robert Ferrers when he rebelled against Henry III in the 13th century and lost his lands to Edmund Plantagenet, Earl of Lancaster.

The Paganell dynasty was only a tad more successful than that of Ansculf. It seems that Ralph Paganell, who inherited the castle in about 1130, married a daughter of Robert Ferrers, 2nd Earl of Derby. Together the bridegroom and his father-in-law set off to support

THE EARLY BARONS OF DUDLEY CASTLE

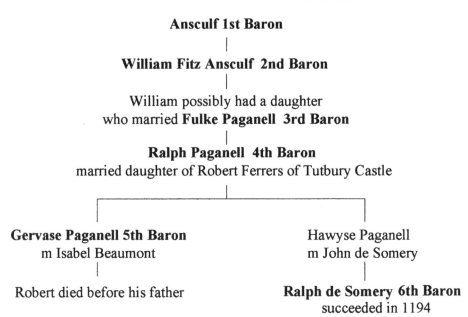

Ansculf 1st Baron

|

William Fitz Ansculf 2nd Baron

|

William possibly had a daughter
who married **Fulke Paganell 3rd Baron**

|

Ralph Paganell 4th Baron
married daughter of Robert Ferrers of Tutbury Castle

|

Gervase Paganell 5th Baron
m Isabel Beaumont

|

Robert died before his father

Hawyse Paganell
m John de Somery

|

Ralph de Somery 6th Baron
succeeded in 1194

Queen Matilda in her struggle against King Stephen. During the following nineteen years of civil strife the barons started to rebuild their castles, so it must have been Ralph who replaced Dudley's wooden fortress with a stone stronghold, adding curtain walls and possibly a gatehouse and drawbridge. Certainly Dudley Castle was robust enough to withstand an onslaught by Stephen's army though the surrounding area suffered terrible devastation with homes and crops burnt and livestock driven away.

During these years the barons continually swapped sides to better their fortunes and it seems that Ralph Paganell was not as adept as his father-in-law at knowing just when to make a move. At any rate, Stephen created Robert Ferrers Earl of Derby for his support, but the owners of Dudley Castle had to wait 409 years and 17 reigns before they received such an accolade.

The last of the Paganells was Gervase, who entertained Matilda's son Duke Henry Plantagenet at Dudley Castle shortly before he became Henry II. But twenty years later Gervase, along with his cousin Robert Ferrers from Tutbury and several other barons, conspired to topple King Henry and place his eldest son on the throne. The rebellion was unsuccessful and the only reason that Gervase and his friends did not lose their heads was that Henry would have had to include his wayward son in the cull. Instead, huge fines were imposed and the offender's castles were all partly demolished so that they were no longer fortresses for the ill-intentioned.

Gervase had no son living at the time of his death and so his sister Hawyse and her husband John de Somery inherited the Dudley barony, along with the unfortified castle. Their great-grandson Roger gave his support to Henry III during the Barons' War of 1264 (when Robert Ferrers lost Tutbury) and the King gave him permission to refortify Dudley Castle. Eventually, the de Somerys, who had been cursed by a lack of sons throughout their tenure of the castle, ran out of male heirs altogether and in 1322 the lands of the barony

The coronation of the first Yorkist king, Edward IV.
The sixth de Sutton baron, John Lord Dudley, lived through seven reigns adding to the family fortunes at every twist and turn. He was born at Dudley Castle in 1400, the year after Henry Bolingbroke usurped the throne to usher in the Lancastrian dynasty as Henry IV. When Edward IV became King, John swapped his allegiance to become a Yorkist. He finally died at the age of 87 in his bed, in the reign of the first Tudor king, Henry VII.

were split between two sisters. The elder, Margaret, inherited a major part of the estates, including Dudley Castle, and so her husband John de Sutton (on Trent) acquired the title.

John de Sutton did not inherit his wife's wealth easily because Hugh Despenser the Younger, that avaricious confidante of Edward II took a shine to the Dudley barony. He contrived to have John imprisoned in the Tower on the basis that he had supported Thomas of Lancaster's rebellion, and he forced him to sign a disclaimer to his estates. After Despenser's execution in 1326, the Dudley lands were held in custody until Edward III became king when John de Sutton was able to petition and regain them.

For the next 170 years the de Sutton barony passed from father to son without much trouble although as they were all named John it gets very confusing. One married Katherine Stafford whose mother was the young heiress kidnapped by Ralph Stafford. Another married Constance, the daughter of Sir Walter Blount, who was killed with Edmund Stafford at the Battle of Shrewsbury fighting the Lancastrian cause. Neither this John's father nor his grandfather owned Dudley Castle, although both were Baron Dudley, because great grandmother Isabella lived to be ninety. She was the daughter of the Lord of Powys and when her husband, John de Sutton II, died she was allowed to keep several of his estates, including Dudley, during her lifetime. When she died, John V was the first Baron Dudley to actually hold the castle for forty years.

The last of the Johns, the sixth de Sutton baron, came into his inheritance when he was six years old in 1406. The little boy grew up to be something of a political mongrel in a way quite alien to his forebears; perhaps the turbulent times, coupled with his pliancy of principle, gave him the opportunity to 'work the system'. He was born at Dudley Castle in 1400, the year after Henry Bolingbroke usurped the throne to usher in the Lancastrian dynasty as Henry IV. He was old enough to fight the French during the next King's reign and carried the standard at Henry V's funeral. During the Wars of the Roses he supported the Lancastrian dynasty and was loyal to the unworldly Henry VI right up until the crown passed to the Yorkist dynasty. He was wounded and captured with King Henry at the battle of St Albans in 1455 and like his 14th century ancestor, did a stint in the Tower. Four years later he fought at the battle of Blore Heath, where leadership of the Lancastrian army fell to him after Lord Audley was killed.

When he was in his early forties he was summoned to Parliament and thus became the first Lord Dudley. In 1460 he was made a Knight of the Garter in recognition of his services to the Lancastrian cause, but the following year, when the crown fell to the House of York and Edward IV became King, he swapped his allegiance to become a Yorkist. He remained loyal to Edward IV's kin while it was expedient to do so and was involved with the Woodvilles in their plans for young Edward V's hurried coronation in 1483. As we know, the coronation never happened. John was acquiescent when Richard III was crowned in his nephew's place and soon afterwards we find John de Sutton, now Lord Dudley, being granted several

Snippet   In 1483 when Richard III lodged the Princes in the Tower the Constable of the Tower was John, Lord Dudley (sixth de Sutton baron). However, John was in his eighties and nearing the end of his long and brilliant career so we can assume that the position was entirely nominal and that he would not have had anything at all to do with the murder of the Princes.

Snippet   Although John, Lord Dudley wasn't at Richard III's coronation, possibly due to his great age, his son and heir Sir Edmund Dudley was there representing the family interests.

John Dudley portrayed with Henry VII and Richard Empson

manors, including Darlaston, Bentley and Bridgnorth, by the grateful King Richard.

He died in his bed in the reign of the first Tudor king, Henry VII. He had successfully manipulated his way through seven reigns, adding to the family fortunes at every twist and turn. At eighty-seven years of age, the wily old baron had outlived his eldest son, and so it was his grandson, Edward, who succeeded him, to be followed by yet another John.

John, Lord Dudley, married Cicely Grey daughter of Thomas Grey, who was the son of Queen Elizabeth Woodville (wife of Edward IV, Chapter 4). John probably had, in today's parlance, 'learning difficulties' as he was incapable of coping with the responsibilities of a medieval landowner and described as 'weak of understanding'. There was, however, a distant relative who was more than capable of administering the Dudley estates. He was Sir John Dudley.

We now need to go back a few generations - the family tree is worth a little study here. The first Lord Dudley (the one who survived seven reigns and lived to 87) had a second son, John. His son was Edmund, born in 1462 just a couple of years after his grandfather had been created a Knight of the Garter. Edmund was a lawyer and an ambitious twenty-three year old when Henry Tudor invaded England to take Richard III's crown at Bosworth. Perhaps the old Lord Dudley was still bustling about the courts and recommended his grandson to the cash-strapped Henry VII, for Edmund now made his career at court, and his fortune, looking after the royal finances.

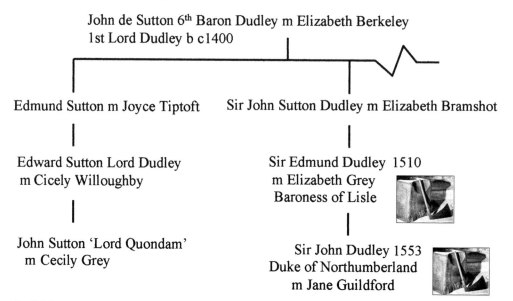

John de Sutton 6th Baron Dudley m Elizabeth Berkeley
1st Lord Dudley b c1400

Edmund Sutton m Joyce Tiptoft

Edward Sutton Lord Dudley
m Cicely Willoughby

John Sutton 'Lord Quondam'
m Cecily Grey

Sir John Sutton Dudley m Elizabeth Bramshot

Sir Edmund Dudley 1510
m Elizabeth Grey
Baroness of Lisle

Sir John Dudley 1553
Duke of Northumberland
m Jane Guildford

The link between Sir John Dudley and the owner of Dudley Castle, Lord Dudley. In the C15th the family started to drop Sutton and assume the name Dudley. John Sutton 'Lord Quondam' and Sir John Dudley were second cousins.

Henry VII's snatched kingdom came with empty coffers and he decided that he stood a better chance of hanging on to it if he managed to become more self-sufficient instead of continually seeking funds from Parliament. Edmund Dudley and Richard Empson helped the King achieve this by implementing various unpopular fiscal measures. For several centuries the nobles had been used to the fact that certain feudal rights of the king were no longer exploited - the levy he was permitted to impose at the knighting of heirs or the marriage of the eldest daughter were examples. Another neglected prerogative involved Tenants-in-Chief and others who were holding property direct from the Crown. The heirs of such tenants were sometimes allowed to succeed to their estates before they were twenty-one although more properly these young people should have become royal wards - as happened to Henry Stafford, 2nd Duke of Buckingham. The Crown would sell the guardianship to the highest bidder who then enjoyed the right to administer his ward's estates and arrange his/her marriage. These neglected sources of income were taken up by Dudley and Empson and the royal revenues increased accordingly.

This whole enthusiastic milking of the nobility, gentry and merchant classes was executed strictly by the book, but this did not make the two chief tax collectors any more palatable to their victims. Empson was derided as the son of a sieve-maker. As for Edmund Dudley, they accused him of fabricating his descent from the House of Dudley when he was the son of a carpenter born in that town - a scurrilous lie.

When Henry Tudor died, his son Henry VIII inherited full coffers and financially wrung-out subjects who insisted that Dudley and Empson had to go. As the two men had worked within the law and at Henry VII's specific bidding, it was not easy to find reasons to punish them; flagrantly trumped up charges were constructed. Edmund was charged with high treason on the basis that he had amassed troops as soon as the King was known to be dying. His intention, his accusers said, was to seize control of the eighteen year old Prince Henry, and through him the government. True, he had probably gathered a few hefty men about him; after all he knew he was just about the most hated man in the kingdom and that his detractors might try to harm him. The indictment of high treason, though, was quite ludicrous. None the less, it stuck and he was executed on Tower Hill in August 1510.

During his years as Henry VII's tax collector, Edmund had become friendly with Sir Edward Guildford, of an ancient family rooted in the south of England. Guildford's father had sailed across the Channel with Henry Tudor's invasion and fought at the Battle of Bosworth. Sir Edward Guildford was permitted to purchase the guardianship of his executed friend's eldest son, John Dudley, aged then about six. The boy was taken from his mother and seven siblings to live in Halden in Kent where he grew up with his guardian's two children, Richard and Jane.

As Edmund had been found guilty of treason he was automatically attainted, which meant that his wealth fell to the Crown. Sir Edward set about having the attainder overturned and he achieved this in a remarkably short time, possibly because Henry VIII knew that the charges against Dudley had been false. It is likely that Sir Edward introduced John Dudley to Court when he was a youth, possibly as a page. When he was nineteen they were fighting in France together and during the campaign John was knighted by Charles Brandon, Duke of Suffolk. A few years later in 1525, the young knight married sixteen year old Jane Guildford, the daughter of his guardian, and she dutifully began producing sons.

By this time Henry VIII was becoming seriously concerned about his own lack of a male heir. Although his wife, Katherine of Aragon, had endured six pregnancies, only one baby had survived, her fifth - and unhappily a girl, Princess Mary. Katherine was now in her forties and unlikely to produce any more children, while Henry had become smitten with one of the Queen's attendants, Anne Boleyn. Unlike other women who had taken the

King's fancy, Anne was not prepared to warm his bed without a wedding ring on her finger, so he decided to rid himself of Katherine.

> Snippet   Henry VIII's wife Queen Katherine of Aragon was the great-great-granddaughter of John of Gaunt and his second wife, Constancia of Castile.

The royal marriage had been sanctioned by a Papal dispensation because she had previously been married to Henry's brother. Although the Queen had failed to provide him with a son, the King's mistress, Bessie Blount, had given birth to a healthy male, Henry Fitzroy. Henry came to reason that the failure to produce an heir with Katherine was a divine punishment - because he had married his brother's widow. According to the biblical text: 'If a man shall take his brother's wife, it is an unclean thing, he hath uncovered his brother's nakedness; they shall be childless'. So Henry asked the Pope to void the dispensation and annul his and Katherine's marriage.

Cardinal Wolsey, Henry's Lord Chancellor, was given the task of achieving this. A year, and a Papal emissary later, Wolsey had failed - it was the end of his career, and many of the King's councillors were glad to witness the fall of this high and mighty Cardinal. Amongst the anti-Wolsey supporters were men who deplored the abuses of the church. The Lutherans held that the Pope had acted outside the scope of his spiritual powers when he granted the indulgence for Henry to marry his brother's widow back in 1509. There were other Lutheran protestations that Henry found favour with too: the inordinate delays in obtaining papal sanctions from Rome; the lack of discipline amongst the clergy; the riches of the Church; the far from pious goings-on in some of the monasteries; and the huge amount of money that poured out of England into papal coffers.

Henry allowed these Lutheran sympathisers to gather round him and work their way into church, court and Privy Council. With their encouragement the reformation of the Church of England began, guided by the newly appointed Archbishop Cranmer. In 1533 Cranmer pronounced that the King's marriage to Katherine of Aragon was without force from the beginning. Henry's embracing of the Lutherans did not amount to support for Protestantism; indeed, the King looked upon Protestants as heretics and several were burned at the stake during the latter part of his reign. Whilst he dislodged the Pope and placed himself at the head of the English Church, dissolved the monasteries and generally brought the clergy to heel.... Henry VIII lived and died a Catholic.

Sir John Dudley quietly and assiduously worked at his career while Henry's attempts to free himself of his Queen kept England and, indeed, all Europe in thrall. He seems to have inherited from his grandfather a certain flexibility of moral fibre that allowed him to embrace any trend that would benefit his situation and, in the early 1530s, he nurtured a friendship with Anne Boleyn and her family who were rumoured to be Protestants.

By 1534 when the King ousted the Pope, declared himself Supreme Head of the Church of England and appointed Thomas Cromwell to his Privy Council, John was inclined towards the reformation movement - and a firm friend of Cromwell. He had supported the King's excuse for casting aside Queen Katherine on religious grounds and encouraged the union with Anne Boleyn. He had seen the light - or at least the path of best rewards - and joined the 'Closet Protestants'.

It was about this time that Sir John Dudley learned of Lord Dudley's financial problems. The owner of Dudley Castle had an acute lack of money, partly inherited, but mainly due to his inability to handle finances. Sir John's continued success at court meant that his original family funds were enhanced by royal grants and wardships so that by his late twenties he was a man of considerable wealth. He had the means to alleviate his distant kinsman's problems and in 1532 he negotiated - indirectly - an enormously convoluted mortgage deal with Lord Dudley. Surety against the £6,000 mortgage was Dudley Castle and estates.

In January 1533 Henry VIII married Anne Boleyn who was expecting a child. For reasons of the succession, the baby needed to be born within wedlock, so the marriage went ahead although his marriage to Katherine had not yet been annulled. In September the new Queen gave birth to a daughter who was called Elizabeth - an obvious choice as both of the baby's grandmothers bore that name as well as her Woodville great-grandmother. In the next three years, while Sir John and Jane Dudley continued to enlarge their own family, notably with the birth of a fifth son, Guildford in 1536, Queen Anne suffered a miscarriage and two full-term stillbirths. By this time Sir John had distanced himself from the Boleyns and become chummy with Edward Seymour whose sister Jane had caught the King's eye. Five months after her second stillborn child, Anne's marriage was declared invalid and she was executed for adultery. Eleven days later, the King married Jane Seymour.

Lord Dudley of Dudley Castle slipped deeper into debt, lamenting to all who would listen that Sir John Dudley's business terms were fraudulent. There is little proof that John's dealings with his kinsman were corrupt, a fairer description might be 'thoroughly rapacious'. By 1537, when news filtered through to Dudley Castle that Queen Jane had died following the birth of a son, Lord Dudley was so completely enmeshed in debts that he was obliged to allow a London syndicate to relieve him of his financial worries in exchange for his estates and his castle. The syndicate was acting on behalf of Sir John Dudley who, over the next few years adopted the title Sir John Dudley of Dudley and bought substantial land holdings in Staffordshire and Worcestershire. He also embarked on a huge rebuilding programme at the castle. The remains of his splendid mansion are still there today.

1537 was an altogether successful year for John. His family continued to grow and thrive, he attended the christening of the motherless heir to the throne, Prince Edward, and he was appointed Vice Admiral. This was his first position of note and although he was not a sailor he went to sea -which was not necessary - and captured a few pirate vessels in the Channel. He became hooked on all things maritime and for the rest of his life kept a finger on the pulse of the country's emerging navy.

Snippet   In 1543 John was appointed Lord Admiral. He showed his nautical flair in 1545 when he repulsed an attempted invasion of the south coast by the French though the occasion was marred by the loss of his vice-flagship, the recently famous *Mary Rose,* which sank within sight of land, drowning nearly 600 men.

When the King married Anne of Cleves in 1540, Sir John Dudley of Dudley was appointed her Master of the Horse. However, John soon saw that Cromwell was out of favour with the King after orchestrating this disastrous marriage and he distanced himself, surviving unscathed when the unfortunate Cromwell was executed.

Sir John stood on the sidelines as the Duke of Norfolk planted his second kin into the King's bed when Henry VIII married his fifth wife, Katherine Howard. Like Anne Boleyn, sixteen year old Katherine was the Duke of Norfolk's niece. Twenty months later John was

A drawing of Henry VIII in old age, and a painting of Prince Edward.

involved with the enquiry into young Katherine's sexual misdemeanours, and working with him was the Duke of Norfolk who, quick to disown the wretched girl, did nothing to save her from the executioner's axe.

> Snippet   The Act of Attainder that despatched Queen Katherine Howard also made it a treasonable offence for any woman whose previous life had been unchaste to marry the King. It was remarked at the time that there would be very few ladies of the court who had the qualities to become Queen.

But Sir John never had much time for the Duke, a devout Roman Catholic who strongly opposed him as one of the King's 'new men' of 'ignoble birth', and when Henry VIII, still smarting from his late wife's antics, imprisoned Howard for spurious treasonable offences, Dudley helped the proceedings along, relieved to have one less enemy at court. By now John was wholly committed to the religious reformers' cause - how much for political gain and how much through belief is impossible to say. He did very well out of the dissolution of the monasteries, gaining Dudley Priory along with other choice blocks of monastic real estate.

In 1542 Sir John became Viscount L'isle by right of his mother Elizabeth Grey. It was the first of a string of titles. The following year, aged forty-one, he was appointed to the Council and admitted to the Order of the Garter. That year, John busied himself promoting Catherine Parr as the King's sixth wife. The Parrs were great friends of the Dudleys and shared religious leanings; in fact the King's last wife was a 'closet protestant'.

When the King of Scotland died in December 1542 leaving as Queen his week old daughter Mary, a marriage treaty between Prince Edward of England and Queen Mary of Scotland was quickly secured. At this time it was noted by a visiting ambassador that Lord L'isle was one of the King's closest councillors.

King Henry was now sick, overweight, virtually immobile and tormented with pain from a leg ulcer.   Nearly twenty years after he had decided to divorce his first Queen he still had only one legitimate son and two illegitimate daughters - even his illegitimate son Henry Fitzroy had died. The two daughters had been declared illegitimate. So much rested on Prince Edward marrying and having sons, yet he was still only a boy and not robust.

In 1544 Parliament's answer to the predicament was to pass an Act that allowed the monarch to bequeath his Crown in his will. The succession stood as follows:

Prince Edward

Princess Mary (Katherine of Aragon's daughter).
Declared illegitimate by Act of Parliament.

Princess Elizabeth (Anne Boleyn's daughter).
Declared illegitimate by Act of Parliament.

Mary Stuart (Queen of Scots).
Grand-daughter of Henry's elder sister, Margaret, wife of the King of Scotland.
Margaret Douglas, Countess of Lennox.
Daughter of Henry's elder sister Margaret by second husband the Earl of Angus.

Lady Frances Brandon.
Daughter of Henry's younger sister Mary Rose
by her second husband, Charles Brandon* Duke of Suffolk.

Ladies Jane Grey, Catherine Grey and Mary Grey.
Lady Frances Brandon's daughters.

* This is the Charles Brandon, Duke of Suffolk, who knighted the 19 year old John Dudley on campaign in France.

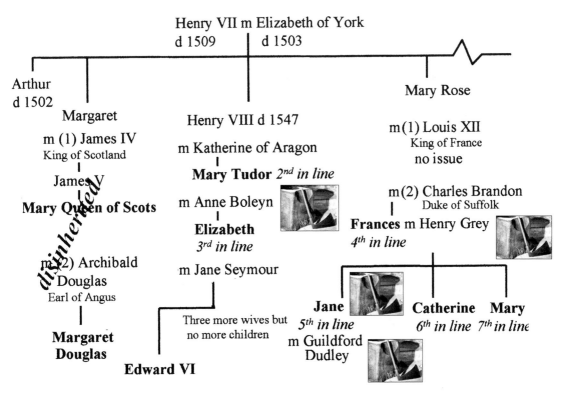

The line of succession according to Henry VIII's will.

This was Henry's incredible dilemma. If Prince Edward did not survive, the next eight heirs were all female. Henry made his last will in December 1546 and appointed sixteen executors. Several of these men, including John Dudley, were at least Reformers, if not downright Protestants.

Taking up the option that Parliament granted him, Henry bequeathed his kingdom, first, to his son Edward and his heirs. Next, to his daughter Mary on condition that she did not marry without the consent of the Council. Next, to his daughter Elizabeth with the same embargo. He then skipped his elder sister's progeny - the Scots connection, and named his younger sister Mary Rose's daughter, Frances Grey (nee Brandon), and then to her daughters, the eldest of whom was Lady Jane Grey.

On 28th January 1547 Henry VIII died. His son, Edward, was nine and a half years old and possessed a phenomenal intellect that his step-mother Queen Catherine Parr had encouraged him to expand. He had been schooled along with several children whose fathers were at court, including Robert Dudley, the fourth of Sir John Dudley's five sons. It is likely that both Princess Elizabeth and Lady Jane Grey would on occasions have been amongst this select group of youngsters, .

Three days into the reign of young Edward VI the executors of his father's will met in the Tower of London and thrashed out a Regency government. Edward Seymour, who was the dead Queen Jane Seymour's brother - the King's uncle, was given the offices of Lord Protector of the Realm and Governor of the King's person.

Within the week, a Privy Council was up and running and the men who were to govern the realm adorned themselves with new honours. Edward Seymour became Duke of Somerset, William Parr became Marquis of Northampton and John Dudley became Earl of Warwick and was appointed Lord Great Chamberlain. These men were all Reformers, waiting to embrace Protestantism as soon as it was politically safe to do so.

Seymour and Dudley were friends as well as political colleagues and they worked closely with Archbishop Cranmer to reform the Church of England. Of necessity it was a gradual process; these changes would have been considered heresy in the previous reign and their instigators burned at the stake.

Not all of the King's advisors were in agreement with Seymour and Dudley's plans; Henry FitzAlan, Earl of Arundel, and William, Lord Paget, were just two of the councillors who were unhappy at the reforms. Edward, at ten years of age probably did not have a great deal of understanding about what was going on in his Council and under his seal. But, by the time he had grown into a youth, there is no doubt that he had a strong, though blinkered, grasp of the religious situation within his realm. Seymour and Dudley were both utterly committed to the reformation movement and they had a great deal of access to Edward so they were able to guide his thoughts and his spiritual beliefs. The youth was a willing pupil and speedily developed into a formidable religious bigot determined that his subjects should embrace Protestantism.

Snippet   William 1st Baron Paget who rose to be Lord Chancellor in the reign of Henry VIII was a Staffordshire man. Legend has it that his father was of humble stock from Wednesbury. When Henry VIII closed the monasteries, Lord Paget acquired, amongst other choice real estate, Beaudesert, one of the palaces of the bishops of Lichfield. This residence, greatly enhanced over the centuries, remained the family seat until early in the 20th century.

The King's half-sister, Princess Mary, had been reared a Roman Catholic and like her mother, Katherine of Aragon, was deeply religious. Mary considered that her brother was being indoctrinated by his mentors and was so bitterly upset about this that she removed herself from Court. Henry VIII had given her the lands that had belonged to the Duke of Norfolk before his fall from favour. She retreated to Thomas Howard's newly built mansion at Kenninghall in Norfolk while the Duke fretted in the Tower waiting for the wheel of political fortune to turn. At Kenninghall she lived quietly, practising her faith and taking virtually no part in England's politics.

During the next two and a half years the Protector, Seymour, struggled to hold the kingdom together. He was at loggerheads with France and Scotland, while at home his religious innovations and his agrarian policy were causing dissent and resentment. He had not managed to secure Edward's marriage to Mary Queen of Scots, even though Henry had been so keen on this match. The Scots had betrothed their five year old Queen to the Dauphin and packed her off to live in France.

In the summer of 1549 several counties rose in rebellion against the Protector's rule. Different areas were rebelling for different reasons; some had social and economic grumbles rooted in land enclosures and others had religious misgivings.

John Dudley spent July securing the City of London and then made his way to the Midlands to protect his estates there. Gradually, the risings were brought under control with forces raised by local gentry. However, in Norfolk, since the fall of the Howards, there was no major family in the county with sufficient authority to mobilise an army. True, Princess Mary was at Kenninghall only twenty miles from the headquarters of the rebel Robert Kett and could have become a figurehead but she refused to get involved.

The Protector sent William Parr to quieten things down but he was unable to disperse the 12,000 strong gathering and eventually Seymour ordered his ally John Dudley to intervene. John took his Midlands army and headed for East Anglia. The battle of Dussindale was a rout and saw an estimated slaughter of 2,000 rebels. John ordered the ringleaders to be hanged - about fifty in all - but he did not allow his soldiers to wallow in a bloodbath of revenge killings. He seemed to have some sympathy with the rebels and blamed the Protector's policies for the spilling of so much English blood. From that time on, the ties of friendship and the close political relationship between this pair fell apart.

John returned to London without dismissing his troops and immediately joined other disgruntled councillors in a bid to overthrow Seymour. By early October the Protector realised that there was a conspiracy against him and that his enemies were amassing troops. He and the King were at Hampton Court with insufficient soldiers to protect them against an attack so he decided to make for Windsor Castle, taking young Edward with him, apparently against his wishes. He wrote to his former comrade, Dudley, reminding him of their friendship, but Dudley did nothing and within a few days Seymour surrendered and was taken to the Tower.

John stepped into his former colleague's shoes and although he shunned the title of Protector he was, from October 1549, the realm's chief political adviser and Edward VI's most trusted councillor. He introduced allies onto the Council including his brother Andrew and a distant cousin Henry Grey, Marquis of Dorset.

Eventually various charges were brought against the former Protector and although he was acquitted of treason he was executed early in 1552. There is no doubt that his removal from the scene benefited John Dudley and from this time the mortar that cemented his political career was Edward Seymour's blood.

During the early 1550s Dudley made a reasonably good job of ruling England although the Catholics were most unhappy at his continued religious reforms. It was grumbled that the King was far too influenced by Dudley, allegations which were, of course, quite true. John knew that his charge was growing up fast and that in five years time he would take over the reins of government. Favours, gifts and continued office would fall to those who had helped and guided the King through his minority and John intended to be at the head of the queue. In the meantime, in 1551, he gave himself a little sop to be going on with - the Dukedom of Northumberland.

John Dudley,
the Duke of Northumberland

John Dudley is often accused of having been driven by ambition but there is no reason to think that he aspired to create a royal Dudley dynasty until the King became terminally ill in the early part of 1553. Until then, John had been doing very nicely - especially as there were still those who insisted that he was the grandson of a Dudley artisan. His creation as Duke of Northumberland was without precedent for never before had anyone without royal blood or marriage ties to royalty been given a dukedom. Having achieved that, there was nowhere higher for him to go; his concerns would have been to increase the family wealth and sustain his position as the King's most trusted friend and adviser.

In the spring of 1552 the King suffered a bout of either smallpox or measles, but probably not both even though his journal records 'I fell sike of the mesels and the smallpokkes.' He never fully recovered from this illness and by the winter it was known that he was suffering from tuberculosis. In the following February when Princess Mary came to visit, John Dudley was sufficiently worried about the youth's health to greet Mary personally at the gates of Westminster Palace with a great deal of bowing and scraping. She was, after all, heir to the throne and it was beginning to look very much as though her brother was not going to live long enough to beget the heirs that would disinherit her.

It has been said that John did not grasp the nettle to secure his position when it was realised that the King's illness was terminal but he was himself a sick man. During the previous five years there had been several instances when he had failed to attend Council meetings because of unspecified maladies. Whatever the reason, John did not act positively quickly enough. He finally started putting a survival plan into action in May 1553 when he married his son Guildford to Lady Jane Grey.

The marriage between Lady Jane Grey and Guildford Dudley was utterly devoid of romantic motivation. Jane was a serious 15 year old with a good helping of the formidable Tudor intellect; Guildford was tall, good looking, spoiled and shallow. The pair were the victims of a religious and political upheaval spawned a quarter of a century before they were born. Of the two, Guildford was possibly even more an innocent victim than Jane, for she must surely have been aware that her royal connections coupled with her Protestantism might perhaps propel her onto the throne if Edward VI died. No wild notion of kingship could ever have entered 17 year old Guildford's head before he learned of the hurried marriage plans his father had made for him. Guildford was marrying Jane because his father said so and, although he had been reared in a Protestant household, there is nothing to suggest he had Jane's enthusiasm for the new religion. His older brother Robert had been allowed to choose his own bride, comely and cheerful Amy Robsart. It was all quite unfair... and it was about to become much more so.

By the time the marriage took place on 21 May 1553, a splendid ceremony at the Dudley's London home, Durham Place, the King was too ill to attend. While Jane and Guildford very quickly discovered a mutual dislike of each other, Edward VI put the finishing touches to the will that was to seal their fate. From the time that he was able to comprehend the religious ramifications of his sister Mary succeeding to the throne, the young King had been worried for his realm. It was a worry that John Dudley shared, though probably for a far more selfish reason. The King knew that Mary would return the country to Roman Catholicism - Dudley knew that Mary would put his head on the block for having encouraged and guided her brother's Protestant leanings. Mary Tudor must never be Queen.

Edward had written - in his own hand, a 'Device for the Succession' early in 1553. His Device barred his two half sisters from succeeding to the throne on the basis that they were both illegitimate. He was concerned also that they might marry a foreigner who would become King and so turn England into a satellite of some foreign Roman Catholic nation. He followed his father's example in ignoring his elder aunt's issue and settled instead on the descendants of his father's younger sister Mary Rose Brandon. This branch of the family was Protestant but there was no male stock - so his device bequeathed the kingdom to the males that might be born to Mary Rose Brandon's daughter, Frances Grey, and then the males to be born to Frances' eldest daughter, Lady Jane Grey.

As Edward's condition worsened, Dudley was forced to accept that his power was about to crumble. Forget high-minded ideas of protecting the Protestant faith; forget preserving his place at the centre of power; forget dreams of a Royal Dudley dynasty; John Dudley was scheming for his life now. Neither Frances Grey, nor her eldest daughter Lady Jane had time to produce a male heir. The dying Edward was persuaded to alter the Device to give succession directly to Lady Jane Grey. The forced marriage between Guildford Dudley and Lady Jane Grey can now be clearly seen for what it was.

It was not easy for Dudley to get the members of the Privy Council, the Lord Mayor of London and Thomas Cranmer, Archbishop of Canterbury, to accept the King's 'tweaked' device and he was reduced to harsh, bullying tactics before the Lord Chief Justice agreed to draw up the required documentation.

Within three weeks of naming Jane Grey - or more correctly Jane Dudley - as his heir, Edward VI died. Dudley had sent a pressing message to Princess Mary at Hunsdon in Hertfordshire, telling her that her brother's life was slipping away. Again, John seems to have tarried when he should have made a decisive effort to lure her to London. Mary set off to make her peace with her brother, but within hours she was warned that there was a trap to capture her and made her way instead, via back roads and safe houses, to her Norfolk estate at Kenninghall. Dudley sent two of his sons, John and Robert, with a retinue of soldiers to escort the Princess into London. When the brothers realised that Mary's retinue were nowhere to be found along the road to the city, they faced a quandary. There was no quick way of contacting their father to find out how he wanted them to handle this very difficult situation. If they chased after the Princess and caught up with her, what were they to do then? She had obviously turned away from London and certainly would not return with them to Greenwich of her own volition. Should they allow her to flee - or capture her? John went back to London to take instructions from his father while Robert took the troops in pursuit.

By the 8th July, the King had been dead for two days and it was impossible for Dudley to suppress the knowledge any longer in the hopes that his sons would bring in Princess Mary. He made an official announcement to the Lord Mayor and the City's aldermen, informing them of the King's death and his daughter-in-law, Jane Dudley's accession to the throne. These men were sworn to secrecy while John awaited news from his sons that Mary was safely in their control.

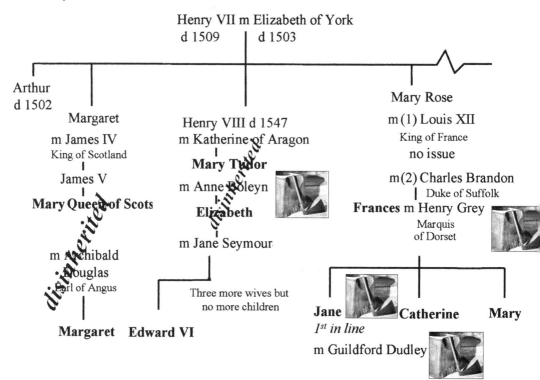

The line of succession according to Edward VI's tweaked 'device' for the succession.

The next day, Jane was summoned to a meeting at Syon House, a splendid riverside manor at Brentford. There she found her detested husband waiting to welcome her along with her equally detested mother-in-law, her own parents, leading members of the Council including the Earl of Arundel, Lord Paget and her father-in-law. John Dudley, Duke of Northumberland greeted her in his capacity as President of the Council. If her total lack of insight into the grand machinations of her elders is true, as she later insisted, then John Dudley's next remarks must have been truly mind numbing. She was told that Edward VI was dead and that he had bequeathed his kingdom to her. She protested, but her power-hungry parents ignored her pleas and her father-in-law, with his back to the wall, certainly was not about to allow a fifteen year old's finer feelings get in the way of his plans.

In accordance with custom, Jane was moved next day into the Tower of London to begin her reign. Her father-in-law, her husband, her father and several members of her Council moved into the fortress with her. Even though Princess Mary was still at large, the country could not be kept in limbo any longer and Dudley had no option but to have Jane proclaimed as Queen of England.

Princess Mary had by the 10th July outwitted her pursuers and arrived safely at Kenninghall where she found East Anglian nobles and gentry eager to help her. Encouraged by this support in a largely Protestant area of England, she wrote to the Council, reprimanding them for not having told her of the King's death and insisting that she be recognised as Queen. As the messenger carried her letter towards London, members of the nobility and the heads of influential families galloped away from the City in the direction of East Anglia, eager to distance themselves from the Dudley dynasty and swear their allegiance to Henry VIII's elder daughter.

John Dudley had not only misjudged the timing of Mary's capture, but also the strength of the loyalty she would attract. As stories of her burgeoning support grew, his Council realised that for the accession of Queen Jane to stand any chance at all of succeeding, it was paramount that Mary should be brought to London and confined in the Tower. The councillors were now desperately regretting their allegiance to Dudley. They decided that Jane's father, Henry Grey, Marquis of Dorset, should take an army into East Anglia to accomplish what their leader's two sons had failed to do. Jane, however, wouldn't hear of her father heading the troops and insisted that he stay with her in the Tower. She was, after all, Queen and so the Council decided that Dudley should command the royalist army instead.

Dudley was not happy. He knew that he needed to be where he could keep a firm grip on his nervous councillors and chivvy the faint hearted into renewed loyalty. The Council though, was adamant. John had allowed this situation to develop by not making sure of Mary's captivity sooner and on top of that, it was his sons who had let her slip through their fingers. Besides, they assured their President, it made sense for him to lead the troops as he was without doubt England's finest commander and after quelling Kett's rebellion four years before, the people of East Anglia remembered him with fear and respect. They promised also, to send him reinforcements as a matter of urgency.

On 14th July, Dudley led his army north-east out of London in search of Mary. The convoy was watched by near silent bystanders. Those who stood to stare had not been happy with King Henry's treatment of his gentle, pious daughter and they regarded her with affection. Their sullen attitude made the popular feeling quite clear to Dudley and his commanders; Queen Jane's subjects were obstinately indifferent to religious or political schemes.... they wanted the Princess Mary to wear her father's crown.

Within a few days of leaving the capital John realised how right he had been to nurse reservations about leaving his councillors. The promised reinforcements did not arrive. Then he learned that the navy, sent to guard the East Anglian coast against any attempt by Mary to escape to the continent had, instead, declared their loyalty for her. This was a huge blow. The newborn Dudley dynasty could not afford for Mary to escape abroad where she could whip up enthusiasm and finances for her cause.

As it turned out, Mary had no need to flee. The Earl of Arundel, Lord Paget and several other members of the Council who were with Jane in the Tower, informed their young Queen that they had urgent business to attend to in the city and took leave of her. Once outside, they declared publicly for Queen Mary and then set off to swear their allegiance to her.

That evening, 19th July, Jane's father slipped out of the Tower and proclaimed Mary Queen. He then returned to his daughter, told her that her reign was over and tore down the canopy of state draped above her chair. The next day she was stripped of her official jewels and taken from the royal apartments to less sumptuous accommodation within the Tower.

Dudley and his sons were rounded up and taken back to London to await trial. Although John's outward journey had been something of an ordeal, it was nothing to the nightmare ride back into the City. Queen Mary had requested that his 'homecoming' should be low-key, but her subjects were not to be denied their sport and as he and his family and supporters were escorted to the Tower, they were booed and pelted with filth.

The Tower of London.

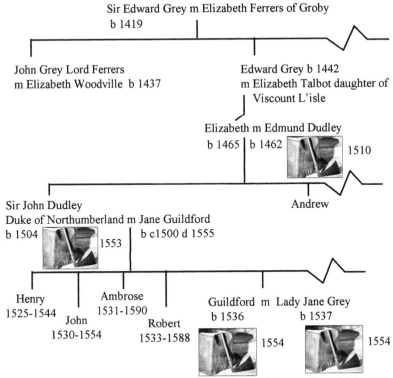

Sir Edward Grey m Elizabeth Ferrers of Groby
b 1419

John Grey Lord Ferrers
m Elizabeth Woodville b 1437

Edward Grey b 1442
m Elizabeth Talbot daughter of
Viscount L'isle

Elizabeth m Edmund Dudley
b 1465 | b 1462   1510

Sir John Dudley
Duke of Northumberland m Jane Guildford
b 1504   1553   b c1500 d 1555

Andrew

Henry
1525-1544

John
1530-1554

Ambrose
1531-1590

Robert
1533-1588

Guildford m Lady Jane Grey
b 1536   b 1537
1554   1554

Two family trees showing (top) the distant relationship by marriage of John Dudley
to Elizabeth Woodville, Queen of Edward IV and (bottom) the blood relationship of Lady Jane Grey and
the Suttons of Dudley to Elizabeth Woodville.

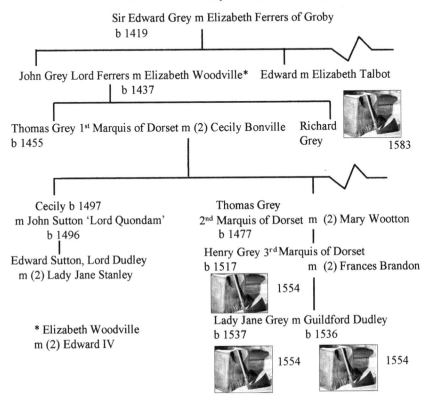

Sir Edward Grey m Elizabeth Ferrers of Groby
b 1419

John Grey Lord Ferrers m Elizabeth Woodville*   Edward m Elizabeth Talbot
b 1437

Thomas Grey 1st Marquis of Dorset m (2) Cecily Bonville   Richard
b 1455   Grey   1583

Cecily b 1497
m John Sutton 'Lord Quondam'
b 1496

Edward Sutton, Lord Dudley
m (2) Lady Jane Stanley

Thomas Grey
2nd Marquis of Dorset m (2) Mary Wootton
b 1477

Henry Grey 3rd Marquis of Dorset
b 1517   m (2) Frances Brandon
                1554

Lady Jane Grey m Guildford Dudley
b 1537   b 1536
1554   1554

* Elizabeth Woodville
m (2) Edward IV

Even John's wife was arrested and lodged in the Tower though she was soon released. She spent the rest of her life trying to persuade Queen Mary to give her five sons their freedom though, of course, for her husband there was no hope of redemption. On 18th August John stood trial. The jury was made up of his fellow peers and led by Thomas Howard, Duke of Norfolk, fresh from the Tower where he had spent the whole of Edward VI's reign under sentence of death. Mary, who had made such good use of the Duke's estates while he was in prison, released him as soon as she became Queen. Now, the old man was in a position to bring low John Dudley who had cost him seven years confinement.

John didn't go without a fight. He apologised for having offended Queen Mary and offered her his loyalty. Had she been prepared to forgive him and accept his allegiance, there is no doubt that John, who was first and foremost a careerist, would have switched political and religious ideals to serve his new mistress as diligently as he had served her half brother and her father. But Mary would have none of it; John Dudley, Duke of Northumberland had to go.

So the man who had carried out his plans after receiving the authority of his fellow councillors was judged to be guilty of treason by those very men. He was to be executed on 21st August but, almost certainly in an attempt to save his life, rather than his soul, John asked to be allowed to denounce his protestant beliefs and revert to Roman Catholicism. Queen Mary was happy enough to oblige him in this request and a great deal of political and religious kudos was wrung from the whole unseemly affair. John's execution was delayed for a day so that his deliverance back into the true faith could be achieved in grand style and well reported. He attended an elaborate mass at the chapel of St Peter ad Vincula within the precincts of the Tower and publicly renounced his religious beliefs of the past sixteen years. The next day, his scaffold recantation in front of several thousand spectators on Tower Green was said to have caused many to readopt Roman Catholicism.

He was spared the final indignity of having his head displayed on a spike and both parts of his decapitated corpse were received in the chapel where he had so recently gambled his soul for his life. In his final resting place before the high altar, he was flanked by two headless Queens, Anne Boleyn and Katherine Howard, who already had one new companion for eternity: Dudley's victim, the Protector Edward Seymour.

John died without knowing Queen Mary's intentions for his daughter-in-law Jane, although her move into the Gentleman Gaoler's house within the Tower grounds gave the impression that she would possibly survive the audacity of her nine days reign. His sons John, Ambrose, Robert, Guildford and Henry were all still imprisoned in the Tower. During their father's last hours there was nothing about the wilful but charming Robert to suggest that the young man would yet secure the Dudley name a place in history as romantic as his father's was tragic.

Chapter 6
A Dud for All Seasons:
Robert Dudley, Earl of Leicester

When the great John Dudley, Duke of Northumberland, sent two of his sons to escort Princess Mary Tudor into London, the young men were fully aware of the importance of their task. It was vital that the King's elder half-sister should be safely tucked away in the Tower while the fledgling Dudley dynasty took root.

The fact that Robert and his elder brother John, Earl of Warwick, were unable to accomplish their task undoubtedly altered the course of history. When they realised that Princess Mary had taken fright and turned her entourage towards Norfolk, they knew that it would be impossible to bring her into London peaceably. And they had no contingency plans from their father.

> Snippet When John Dudley became Duke of Northumberland, his eldest son John took the title Earl of Warwick, his second son Ambrose became Viscount L'isle and the younger sons became Lords Robert, Guildford and Henry.

Perhaps if Robert had gone back to London for fresh instructions and John had continued on Mary's trail the outcome of the events between 6th and 19th of July 1553 might have been different. But it was John, the elder, calmer and less flamboyant who returned to London while his twenty year old brother took their army in pursuit of Mary.

This was the first time that Robert had been in charge of troops since he commanded a small company of foot soldiers during his father's famous handling of Kett's rebellion. Robert had no senior officers advising him this time and he was aware that many of his men were sympathetic towards Mary. His confidence would already have been shaken, aware that he and John had failed their father by not delivering the Princess to London. It was up to him to locate Mary and he did not know what support she had or how deeply into East Anglia she had travelled. He must find her and hang on to her until his brother returned with fresh instructions from their father.

Robert arrived in Cambridge during the early hours of the morning and learned that the Princess had not been there. He found out that she was heading for her estate at Kenninghall and was moving across country via friendly houses such as Sawston Hall. Sawston was seven miles south and slightly to the east of Cambridge. Robert, after a very brief rest, set off again. He arrived at John Huddlestone's fine moated manor house as dawn broke and learned that his quarry had left there in the direction of Newmarket just an hour or so before. Mary wasn't that far in front of him and yet, incredibly, Robert lingered long enough to set Sawston Hall on fire. It was a time consuming act of mindless vandalism which gave Mary the chance to disappear and ultimately to arrive at Kenninghall on 6th July, the day that Edward VI finally died.

Robert found it increasingly difficult to hold his troops together as rumours of the King's death spread, and an upsurge of loyalty for Princess Mary swept across East Anglia. The men became disruptive and disrespectful towards their young leader. Cowed and

Legend has it that when Mary looked back and saw the flames of Sawston Hall she vowed
that she would rebuild John Huddlestone's home for him. A few years afterwards,
a fine new manor house replaced the charred ruins. *Courtesy of Dr Roger Joy.*

irresolute, Robert retreated to Cambridge to wait for his brother. When John arrived with
confirmation of Edward VI's death, they set off again towards Newmarket but as they
advanced into hostile territory the soldiery abandoned them at such a rate it became unsafe
to continue. They separated with the intention of raising more troops and Robert spent the
next ten days canvassing for support in the areas of Norfolk where his father-in-law owned
estates. He achieved some success and on 18th July he proclaimed his sister-in-law Lady
Jane Grey as Queen in Kings Lynn. He then waited for reinforcements to arrive.

Two days before, Robert's father arrived in Cambridge at the head of a resentful and
belligerent army much reduced by desertions. Since setting out from London John Dudley
had learned of the navy's defection and on the day that Robert proclaimed Jane Queen, he
received the news he had been half expecting, that the Council had abandoned the Tower and
declared for Mary. The great Duke of Northumberland rode into the centre of Cambridge
and there proclaimed Henry VIII's eldest daughter as Queen Mary.

By the time Mary's soldiers arrived in Kings Lynn to arrest Robert he knew that the
Dudley coup had failed. He was taken to the Queen's headquarters at Framlingham Castle in
Suffolk and there he threw himself on her mercy, promising loyalty and service. Although
many of the Duke of Northumberland's accomplices had already been pardoned, the Queen
was not ready to look upon the Dudleys with clemency and he was sent to the Tower.

Five of Jane Dudley's sons had survived the dangers of a medieval infancy and the
uncertainties of war, now they had to survive Mary Tudor's wrath. They were lodged

together in the Beauchamp Tower within the Tower of London where they whiled away idle hours carving into the stonework.

Snippet   The Beauchamp Tower where John Dudley's five sons were imprisoned was named after a former inmate Thomas Beauchamp, Earl of Warwick who was imprisoned there while he awaited trial in 1397. He was one of the Lords Appellant and subsequently a victim of Richard II's tyranny.

Their father was imprisoned in the Garden Tower - now known as the Bloody Tower - where Richard, Duke of Gloucester, and Henry, Duke of Buckingham, had imprisoned the two princes 70 years before. It is unlikely that his sons saw him again until the 21st August, the day set for his execution. The brothers were taken to the chapel of St Peter ad Vincula within the Tower precincts where an impressive array of dignitaries was assembled. Dudley, his brother Andrew, William Parr and other men under sentence of death for their part in the attempt to divert the succession, were led into the chapel. Bishop Gardiner performed a full Roman Catholic service and the men who were to die received the sacrament. Then, John Dudley turned to the congregation and denounced the protestant faith that he had so diligently thrust upon the English people. This painful and humiliating scene was the last time Robert saw his father.

Snippet   Although John Dudley's brother Andrew and William Parr were tried and found guilty of high treason they were not executed and eventually both were given their freedom.

Three months later it was Guildford's turn to face official vengeance. He and Jane, along with others of the Dudley clan, were put on trial for high treason. They all pleaded guilty to the charges and were sentenced to death. Queen Mary, however, was reluctant to sign their death warrants and they remained in the Tower, uncertain of their fate. Jane, in fact, was not actually in prison, for she was living with the Gentleman Gaoler and his wife in their house overlooking Tower Green. Mary accepted that the young girl was nothing but a pawn in John Dudley's dynastic plans and she had let Jane know that she would eventually be given her freedom.

The Dudley brothers would have heard that Jane's life was to be spared. This would have been encouraging news - the queen was beginning to thaw. For the time being though, while she was so wrapped up in her marriage negotiations with Philip of Spain, the brothers could only wait and hope that nothing happened to change her mind.

In January 1554 the last of the Dudleys was brought to trial - Robert. The reason for the delay seems to have been that his treasonable offences took place in and around Norfolk and so evidence had to be sought in that area. Like his brothers, he pleaded guilty as charged and was sentenced to death.

In that same month Kent rose in rebellion against the Royal Spanish marriage with its political and religious implications. The rebels were led by a Protestant, Sir Thomas Wyatt, whose intention was to place the Protestant Princess Elizabeth on the throne in place of Catholic Mary. This was just the sort of trouble that the Dudley brothers had feared. Any disturbance that threatened Mary's throne could cause a panic that would result in a complete clear-out of the Tower.

The rebels marched on London but were overwhelmed by royalist troops - Wyatt surrendered and his huge following dispersed. At the same time, in the Midlands, another insurgence in support of Wyatt failed to get off the ground. It was led by Jane's father

Lady Jane Grey

Henry Grey, Duke of Suffolk. In the wake of the Dudley coup, Grey had been imprisoned but surprisingly, Mary had set him free. He was not treated leniently a second time, and to let her subjects know that she would not tolerate political and religious dissent, Mary signed his death warrant and the long outstanding warrants for Jane and Guildford.

This was horrific news for the Dudley brothers, although Robert would perhaps have felt Guildford's distress more acutely than John, Ambrose and Henry. In 1550 when he was seventeen he had married his sweetheart Amy Robsart, while three years later his brother at seventeen had been thrust into the loveless union that was now to cost him his life.

On 12th February, at 10 o'clock, Guildford followed in the footsteps of his father and his grandfather when he was taken out to Tower Hill for a public execution. His four brothers would not have been able to see the sombre little procession from their prison quarters in the Beauchamp Tower, but Jane had an uninterrupted view as she stood at the window of her lodgings in the Gentleman Gaoler's house. She watched her husband walk to his death and she watched the cart lumber his truncated body back for burial in the chapel of St Peter ad Vincula. Within hours, Jane's headless corpse followed Guildford's into the chapel. But they were not buried together; Jane was placed with two other Queens who had fallen foul of a Tudor monarch, Anne Boleyn and Katherine Howard.

Henry Grey was executed later that month. In the meantime, Queen Mary's half sister Princess Elizabeth was arrested on the basis that she had been in collusion with the protestant rebels. She was taken by barge to the grim Tower fortress where her mother, Anne Boleyn, had met her end. Her lodgings were on an upper floor of the Bell Tower not far along the curtain wall from the Beauchamp Tower where a companion of her youth was still awaiting his fate - Robert Dudley.

Robert was no stranger to royalty and contrary to popular myth, he and Princess Elizabeth did not meet for the first time in the Tower of London. By the time Robert was seven his father had moved his principal seat to the Midlands and adopted the title Sir John Dudley of Dudley, but this did not mean that the family spent much time at the castle - it was too distant from the capital. It was a trophy - to own the castle that bore his name endorsed John's claim as head of the Dudley clan. Robert grew up in and around London. In the winter the family lived at their city home, a grand palace which had belonged to the bishops of Ely before the reformation. In the summer they moved out to Sussex or Kent and maybe occasionally Staffordshire, leaving disease-ridden London to those who had no option but to live there. Robert's father seems to have been very family-orientated and there was never any scandal surrounding his private life; no affairs and no mistresses.

When Henry VIII had married his sixth wife, Catherine Parr, Robert's mother had attended the ceremony as a friend of the bride. Catherine had immediately set about mending the rift that Henry had forced between himself and his daughters. She also made it her business to make sure that the King's two younger children were educated by the best scholars of the day. Jane Dudley's children were invited, along with several other privileged youngsters, to share Prince Edward's education, so Robert knew the heir to the throne from boyhood. During the three and a half years that Catherine was married to the King, Princess Elizabeth occasionally visited her father and at such times, she would have joined the royal classroom. Robert and Elizabeth were the same age and both were extrovert, energetic youngsters with a love of anything to do with horses - so they surely would have been well acquainted.

In 1549 when the South-West and Norfolk were in rebellion, the dissidents, led by Robert Kett, were skirmishing and looting across Norfolk and John Dudley was sent to suppress them. He took with him his sons, Ambrose and Robert. This was sixteen year old Robert's first military campaign and he was given command of a company of foot soldiers, although there would have been experienced officers on hand.

A day or two before the rebels were successfully confronted John Dudley and his commanders were received and entertained at Stanfield Hall by Sir John Robsart, a prominent Norfolk landowner. It was here that Robert first met Amy Robsart. Nothing is known of their courtship, no letters have survived, but their passion for each other was allowed to flourish. John Dudley had promised his older children to partners of powerful families and he could easily have arranged such a match for Robert. Perhaps he was charmed at the thought of this love-match. At any rate, Robert was allowed to marry the girl of his choice.

The wedding took place on 4th June, 1550, at the splendid riverside residence of the King's uncle, the Protector of the Realm, Edward Seymour. On the previous day, at the same venue a much more auspicious marriage had been celebrated when Seymour's daughter Anne had married Robert's eldest brother John. The twelve year old Edward VI had attended both weddings. Although there were grand entertainments and feasting for the first day's nuptials, Robert and Amy's festivities were far less spectacular, but Edward seems to have enjoyed himself nonetheless and reported in his diary *'there were several gentlemen who did strive which should first take away a goose's head which hanged alive on two cross-posts.'*

To have the King attend your wedding was the ultimate accolade. Robert was definitely the King's man. But by June 1553, with the King near to death, the series of events were set to unravel that would see his father and his younger brother executed, and himself lodged in the Beauchamp Tower a self-confessed traitor under threat of execution. His new neighbour in the Bell Tower was equally terrified for her life, though the Princess Elizabeth swore that she was innocent of any treason.

It was more than Queen Mary dared do to have Elizabeth put to death. She realised that the faithful subjects who had risen to insist on her right to be Queen, might rise again if she attempted to tamper with the law of succession by destroying the heir presumptive. The Princess was released from the Tower after two months and sent to live under house arrest at Woodstock in Oxfordshire.

There is no proof that Robert and Elizabeth met while they were both in the Tower - the Princess was kept under very strict surveillance. However, the legend was full blown even in their lifetimes that, not only did they meet, but that Robert Dudley contrived to capture Elizabeth's enduring love during her short captivity.

The Dudley brothers remained prisoners with little hope of release although every day that passed without a date being set for their execution meant that it was less likely. Their mother worked tirelessly to persuade Queen Mary to pardon her sons but it was a humiliating task because nobody at court wanted to be seen associating with Jane Dudley.

Then in the spring of 1554, John, the eldest son, became ill. In the autumn he was freed into the care of his sister Mary and her husband Sir Henry Sydney on condition he lived with them at their Penshurst Manor in Kent. He died within a week of his release and his mother died, broken and embittered just a few months later. Ironically, the order to free her sons, Robert, Ambrose, Henry, and their uncle Andrew, was issued on the day that she died.

At first the Dudleys had their freedom but little else. Their attainders were not lifted, they were virtually penniless and unwelcome at court. But when Queen Mary's husband, King Philip of Spain, required an English fighting force to help in the Spanish conflict against the French, the Dudley fortunes began a slow up-turn. Philip had just taken over the reins of his father's kingdom and Robert was employed as a messenger while the Spanish king toured his continental territories. Robert suggested that if the attainders were lifted from him and his two brothers they would be in a position to raise retainers to fight for Spain. Queen Mary was infatuated with her debonair young husband and could refuse him nothing. So the Dudley brothers were restored to their lands and went off to fight in the Franco-Spanish conflict, where the youngest son, Henry, was killed during the campaign.

Snippet Two of John and Jane Dudley's children were named Henry. The first born Henry died campaigning in France in 1544. It was the second Henry who was killed fighting in France for King Philip of Spain.

The absence of a baby in the royal nursery was nothing short of a tragedy for Queen Mary but good news for all Protestant sympathisers, including Robert. After fighting for Philip he retreated to his wife's Norfolk estates to live the life of a country squire and wait for the ailing and heirless Queen Mary to die. It was not a long wait. She died on the 17th November 1558 having returned England to the Roman Catholic faith, but by now hated by her subjects for her Spanish marriage and her religious persecutions - and knowing that the next monarch would not follow her religious commitment.

Robert was poised ready to act as soon as he received the news. Twenty-five years old, tall, darkly handsome, dressed in the height of fashion astride a pure white horse, he arrived at the new Queen's home, Hatfield House. Queen Elizabeth welcomed him and appointed him Master of the Horse. His first task was to arrange her coronation. Robert Dudley and Elizabeth Tudor had endured and survived; now they were ready to set the world on fire.

Within a month of becoming Queen, Elizabeth's advisors were harassing her to choose a husband and provide the kingdom with heirs. There were all manner of eligible princes in Europe ready to pay court to the young Queen of England and the Council spent much time in those early months deciding who would best suit England's political and religious purposes. It never occurred to this self-appointed matrimonial agency that Elizabeth might not be prepared to fall in with their arrangements.

She sent the marriage-mongers packing with vague excuses - she was already married to her kingdom; she would be happy to die a virgin; God would sort out the succession if she didn't. However, the reason that Elizabeth was not prepared to discuss seriously any of the splendid marriage propositions set before her soon became apparent. She was already committed. By April 1559 the courtiers and councillors were astonished to realise that the Queen and Robert Dudley had some sort of intimate understanding.

Assuming the story of Robert contriving to win Elizabeth's heart while they were both in the Tower is a myth, it may well have been an uncomfortable shock when he first realised that Elizabeth was smitten - how was he supposed to handle the situation? He was a married man!

Even if he and Amy were no longer enamoured of each other, a wife was still an unassailable obstacle to any wild ambitions that the Queen's infatuation for him might awaken. In true Dudley fashion, Robert was prepared to do his best to capitalise on the situation - and who could blame him? A chance to turn back the clock. A chance perhaps, to create a Royal House of Dudley after all.

As for Elizabeth, if she could have made a choice, it seems certain that she would not have fallen for Robert Dudley. His grandfather had been beheaded as a traitor, his father had been beheaded as a traitor and his brother had been beheaded as a traitor. Robert himself had only survived because Queen Mary was less diligent about cutting off the heads of traitors than she was about burning protestants.

Robert Dudley, Earl of Leicester

Elizabeth I

However, matters of the heart have more to do with chemistry than common sense and for Elizabeth, the molecular mix that was Robert Dudley kept her in thrall until the day she died. By the summer of 1559 the love affair was common knowledge in the courts of Europe. That the Queen of England should be contemplating marriage with her Master of the Horse was an amusing, titillating piece of gossip. That her paramour was inconveniently married added spice to the story. As the rumours progressed, they developed and by the autumn two different stories had evolved. The first suggested that Amy was a very sick woman with 'a malady in one of her breasts' which was likely to kill her sooner rather than later and leave Robert free to remarry. The other story

was much more sinister, insinuating that the Queen and her lover were plotting to murder Lady Dudley.

This malignant story seems to have originated with Elizabeth's secretary Sir William Cecil, a man she later came to rely on. Cecil had started his career as a protégé of Sir John Dudley and knew the family well enough to attend Robert's wedding to Amy in 1550. Years later, he was to describe their nuptials as 'a carnal marriage, begun for pleasure and ended in lamentation'. He was probably right on both points. Amy, who was about eighteen at the time of her marriage, failed to mature in tandem with her husband. Robert was thoroughly educated and utterly cultivated while Amy was probably unable to read or write. Two letters that she wrote to Robert have survived the years and in both cases, only the signature is Amy's.

There is nothing unusual in the fact that Amy was not at court with Robert because there were no facilities for courtier's wives at the royal palace unless they were chosen as ladies-in-waiting. However, most of the courtiers had town houses in the city where they entertained in lavish style during 'the season' and were able to see their families on a fairly regular basis. Robert, though, had no such property. It could be that this was simply a matter of finance. His salary as Master of the Horse and other financial perquisites that Elizabeth made available to him would still not have enabled him to maintain a grand London residence. However, it is also probable that Amy was not inclined to live as the mistress of a great house and when Elizabeth gave Robert a house on the Thames at Kew in 1559, Amy chose not to live there. She was a great visitor, living with a female companion named Mrs Odingsells as the house guest of various members of the gentry. Robert's accounts show that there were occasional visits between them. Amy came to London in 1559, possibly for his investiture as a Knight of the Garter. But after that there are no records of travelling expenses to confirm that the couple ever saw each other again.

Maybe it was on the visit to London that Amy learned of her husband's philandering. If so, it is no wonder that she never went to court again. How could she take on the Queen of England? If the Queen wanted Lord Robert, then what was going to happen to the wife who frustrated her desire?

Sir William Cecil mistrusted Robert and was extremely concerned about the political implications of his relationship with the Queen. Dudley was, after all, a convicted traitor, already implicated in an attempt on the throne, and his close friendship with the sovereign was making England the laughing stock of Europe.

In the summer the court had moved to Windsor and there Cecil had a private meeting with the Spanish Ambassador, de Quadra. The ambassador was keeping Philip of Spain (Queen Mary's widower) up to date on the progress of the Queen of England's affair with her favourite, and although he had been sworn to secrecy, de Quadra wasted no time in relaying Cecil's confidences. He reported that the Queen and Dudley were planning to put Lady Dudley to death and that they were spreading the news that she was a very sick woman. Cecil had assured de Quadra that Amy was not in any way ill and that she was taking great care not to be poisoned. Two days later, Amy was found dead at the bottom of the stairs at Cumnor Place with her neck broken.

Except for the Cecil de Quadra allegations, the overwhelming evidence points to the fact that Amy's death was either a tragic accident, suicide or perhaps a cry for help that went wrong. At the time though, panic overtook Robert and Elizabeth as they considered the enormity of Amy's sudden death. As far as Robert's enemies were concerned, and there were many at court that would welcome his downfall, Amy's death was just too convenient.

The lovers realised that they could not afford to be seen fraternising while the cause of Amy's death posed such a huge question mark and Elizabeth banished Robert from Windsor. He was forced to stay in exile at his house at Kew while a Coroner's inquiry set about discovering how Amy had died. The inquest found no reason to assume anything other than accidental death and Dudley was never officially under suspicion. Popular opinion though, has not been so ready to accept his innocence and over four hundred years after Amy Robsart's death there is still debate and surmise over what exactly happened at Cumnor Place on Sunday 8th September, 1560.

Written details of the official inquiry have not survived but Robert instructed one of his retainers to make independent investigations and the letters that Thomas Blount sent to his master at Kew, and Robert's replies, more or less support the official findings.

Nowhere in the correspondence with Blount does Robert express any grief at the loss of his wife or anguish for any suffering she may have endured. Nonetheless, two weeks after her death he gave her an extravagantly expensive funeral and then tried to pick up the pieces of his life. However, the circumstances of his wife's death put the brakes on any marriage plans that he and Elizabeth might otherwise have considered. Hostile opinion and innuendo were rampant at home and about the courts of Europe. Mary Queen of Scots quipped from her French throne that 'by lucky chance' Queen Elizabeth was now free to marry her Horse Keeper.

For Elizabeth this pause in their relationship gave her the chance to gather her strength and determination. Elizabeth was not at all inclined to trust her life and her well-being to a man. Her lack of confidence in men is not at all surprising. For starters, her father had beheaded her mother. It is doubtful that Henry put his little daughter on his knee and tried to justify his actions. Much more likely she picked up the horrific details of Anne Boleyn's death through careless gossip or cruel remarks flung out by her big half-sister Mary.

She would have been about eight before she could possibly have comprehended such bizarre information - just about the time that her father put another Queen to the axe. So Elizabeth learned very early that marriage could constitute a serious hazard.

Then, when she was a teenager, one of the few people to consider her needs and show her human kindness was Henry's last wife Catherine Parr. Four months after the King died, Catherine married Thomas Seymour and took Elizabeth to live with her at Sudeley Castle. Within eighteen months of this marriage, Catherine died in childbirth. Elizabeth learned that for women, the natural consequences of marriage constituted another mortal threat.

And there was more.... the man who married Elizabeth would expect to become King. Her councillors would expect her to make him King. Her subjects would expect her to make him King. But if she bowed to these demands where did that leave her? As a Queen, she would be expected to subjugate herself to her King. She was not prepared to become her King's Consort. So how could she wed this particular man, this ambitious charmer whose blood was tainted with three generations of treachery? Quite simply, she couldn't.

But she couldn't let him go either.

Once the coroner had announced the cause of Amy's death to be misadventure, clearing Dudley's name, Elizabeth recalled him to court. Shortly afterwards papers were drawn up to ennoble him and then, in a fit of pique she shredded the charter in front of him. It was by no means the only occasion when the Queen vented her spleen on Robert who at other times enjoyed spectacular favours - and the endearing nick names of 'Two Eyes' and 'Robin'. Elizabeth could blow hot and cold, grant honours or withhold them, and Robert could do nothing but ride the tiger. Certainly he could not have ended the relationship, even if he had been minded to do so. His future had become hopelessly wrapped up in hers. She refused to allow him to leave court and make a new life for himself just as steadfastly as she refused to marry him. He found himself treading a path every bit as dangerous as the one his father had trodden; for he could no more stop the Queen from loving him than his father could have stopped young Edward VI from dying.

Of course, there were tremendous advantages in being the Queen's favourite and Robert took full advantage accepting land grants and export concessions so that he very quickly became immensely wealthy. Such blatant favouritism did nothing for his popularity and there emerged an anti-Dudley party headed by Thomas Howard, Duke of Norfolk. The animosity between these two men had a lot to do with old family scores.

Although Ambrose was the elder brother, it was Robert who emerged as head of the Dudley clan and as such, he very much desired to own the castle that bore the family name. His father had spent lavishly on rebuilding the residential apartments to the highest and most elegant specification. With the Duke's downfall and the confiscation of his property, the Dudley estates had passed to the crown. Queen Mary restored *the whole castle of Dudley, the park called the Conigre, the Park called the Old Park of Dudley, Rowley and Sedgley'* to Edward, Lord Dudley whose father had allowed it to slip through his fingers.

Robert wrote to Edward asking if he could purchase the castle and estates, but Lord Dudley was not prepared to sell - although he did state in his reply that if he had no heirs, then he would be happy to see Robert inherit it. As his second wife provided him with two sons, Robert had to drop the idea of ever owning Dudley Castle though he always retained strong ties in the Midlands and when the Queen got over her temper tantrum and eventually granted him his Earldom, he chose another Midlands township for this and became Earl of Leicester.

In October 1562 the Queen became seriously ill with smallpox and she was not expected to survive. Eventually, though, the crisis passed and while she was still extremely weak, she called her councillors together and told them that if she did not pull through, Lord Robert was to be appointed Protector of the Realm at a salary of £20,000. She also told them that the relationship between her and Robert had never been anything but chaste....! Soon afterwards Dudley was appointed to the Council and thus he moved officially into the political arena where he had been dabbling - unofficially - for the past four years. In 1563 he was granted Kenilworth Castle which had been annexed to the royal house along with the Duchy of Lancaster back in the reign of Henry IV. He now had a stately seat in the Midlands and he set about rebuilding it just as his father had rebuilt Dudley Castle.

Gradually, after Elizabeth recovered, there appeared a significant lobby supporting

Robert's matrimonial aspirations on the basis that if the Queen would not marry for political or religious advantage, then at least let her marry for love - just so long as she got on with the business of filling the royal nursery. This support from the Council was a welcome turn-around for Robert. If the encouragement had come a year or so earlier, it may have made all the difference to Elizabeth who, until Amy's death, was wearing her heart on her sleeve. Now, although Robert's position as favourite was unassailable, her passion had subsided into something more manageable. Elizabeth was no longer in danger of allowing her heart to rule her head. Although Robert may not yet have realised it, there was to be no marriage, and no Dudley dynasty to rule England. Or was there?

By the spring of 1563 Elizabeth was even able to consider allowing Robert to marry someone else. The woman she had in mind was ten years younger than herself, tall, beautiful and equally able to provide him with a crown. She was also the only woman besides Elizabeth who could plant Dudley genes on the throne of England. It was the Roman Catholic Mary Stuart, Queen of Scotland and dowager Queen of France. She was also, at least in her own opinion, the rightful Queen of England. Of course, Elizabeth did not quite see it that way but she accepted in her heart that as she herself intended to remain unmarried, Mary Stuart's progeny would inherit England. What better then, than to join together the man she loved, but could never risk marrying, with this kinswoman to whom she must leave her kingdom. She would live to see her beloved 'Robin' and her nearest living relative create the son who would rule England. And Elizabeth would sleep more soundly in her bed knowing that Robert Dudley slept in Mary's. Very tidy.

Although Henry VIII had been keen for his son to marry little Mary Queen of Scots, the plans had never materialised and instead, she was packed off to France, as a five year old, to marry the Dauphin. The marriage took place in 1558 when Mary was fifteen and her husband Francis, thirteen. Seven months later when the English Queen Mary Tudor

Kenilworth Castle, Robert Dudley's main seat.

died, the French King declared his daughter-in-law Queen of England on account of the fact that Elizabeth I was illegitimate. As far as the Roman Catholic Church was concerned Henry VIII's daughter by Anne Boleyn was born out of wedlock because Henry's divorce had not been recognised in Rome.

The following year the French King was killed in a jousting tournament. Mary Stuart, already styled Queen of England and Scotland, became Queen of France alongside Francis II. Just over a year later when news of Amy Robsart's suspicious death hit the French court, Queen Mary's gleefully malicious quip did nothing to help relations between the two women. At that time, it would never have occurred to Mary that she might ever need to cultivate Elizabeth's good wishes. But within four months Francis II died leaving his young Queen to the untender mercies of her Valois and Medici in-laws.

The Valois family had no intention of allowing Mary, as dowager Queen, any form of political influence, and in any case, she was neither old enough nor intellectually equipped to forge a niche for herself at the French court against such formidable relatives. Her only hope was to find a new husband to protect her interests as a matter of urgency. The Valois made life so difficult in that respect that she very soon decided to return to the land of her birth and take up her role as Queen of Scotland. Once there she would continue to seek out a husband with the military strength and the political and religious incentive to further her claim to the crown of England.

She sailed from Calais in August of 1561 and as her flotilla crossed the English Channel and entered the North Sea, Elizabeth's ships postured at a discreet distance, a show of hostility towards the woman who had the audacity to call herself Queen of England. It was because Elizabeth accepted that there was a huge grey area surrounding her birthright that she regarded Mary Stuart as such a threat to her crown and even her life. While Mary let her spousal requirements be known across Europe, Elizabeth, her councillors, nobles and supporters watched events closely with a keen and worried interest.

There was one young man in particular whose claim to the English throne made it extremely important that he was not allowed to contemplate marriage with the Scots Queen. He was Henry Stewart, Lord Darnley, who like Mary shared blood ties with Queen Elizabeth that gave him a claim to the English throne. The grandmother of both was Margaret Tudor, sister of Henry VIII. Whereas Mary was descended through Margaret Tudor's first marriage to James IV of Scotland, Darnley was descended through her second marriage to Archibald Douglas, Earl of Angus. Darnley's claim was inferior to Mary's; however, the young man was Protestant and England had returned to Protestantism under Elizabeth, though without the religious zeal of Edward VI's reign. Also in Darnley's favour was the fact that he had been born in England and the English would have found this a comfort in the event of Mary Queen of Scots attempting to become their Queen.

Snippet   Mary Queen of Scots was born a Stewart as was Henry, Lord Darnley. According to J Keith Cheetham in his fascinating book *On the Trail of Mary Queen of Scots* there was no 'w' in the French alphabet in the 16th century, so, at the French court, she learned to spell her name as Stuart. Darnley also adopted the French spelling.

Although neither of them had shown much political acumen, united in matrimony and with the right backing, Mary Stuart and Lord Darnley could have caused Elizabeth a great deal of anxiety and so she refused to grant the young man leave to travel to Scotland. Instead, she created Robert Dudley Earl of Leicester and then offered him to Mary as a husband. Enobling him seems to have been a case of equipping him for the position of King Consort of Scotland.

The Scots' Queen was less than impressed. In fact, she felt herself to be downright insulted that Elizabeth should have offered to unload a cast-off lover in her direction. Robert too, was decidedly unenthusiastic about having to leave London and take up residence in Edinburgh, even though the prize was so glamorous. It may have been that he felt there was still a chance with Elizabeth, while marrying Mary and moving to Scotland would have left the field clear for her other suitors.

While he tarried in England, reluctant to pay court to Mary, the Scots' Queen informed Elizabeth that she was prepared to consider marriage to Dudley only if she was named as heir to the English throne. This Elizabeth was not prepared to do and so negotiations dragged on with Robert being as awkward and uncooperative about the whole matter as he dared. Meanwhile, Lord Darnley again requested permission to visit his father Lord Lennox in Scotland and Robert intervened on his behalf until eventually Elizabeth, in spite of her better judgement, allowed the young man to go. Within a remarkably short space of time he and the Scots Queen met, fell in love and married, which was exactly what Elizabeth had feared might happen - and exactly what Dudley had hoped would happen. Within a year of her marriage, Mary Queen of Scots gave birth to a son, James. 36 years later, in 1603, James Stuart, the only son of Lord Darnley and Mary Queen of Scots, took up the throne that Queen Elizabeth had relinquished in the early hours of 24th March.

The Queen of England had never married and even if Robert Dudley had been prepared to leave her in favour of the Scots Queen, it is very unlikely that she would have filled the void with a husband. It is extremely likely though, that if Robert had acquiesced to Elizabeth's bidding, the new King of England to take up his inheritance would have borne the name Dudley!

A young Mary when she was Queen of France.

Part 4
Mary Queen of Scots
& Dr Roger Joy's replicas of
Mary Queen of Scots'
Embroideries worked by
Sylvia M. Everitt MBE
(with her notes)

Mary Queen of Scots' Embroideries

When my wife Sylvia died in 2000, I cast about for a fitting memorial to her. We had both enjoyed gazing at the Marie Stuart embroideries at Oxburgh Hall on a number of occasions. Therefore, when I saw some of Sylvia Everitt's work I decided to ask whether she'd be willing to create replicas of a small number of these.

Marie Stuart grew up at a time when every noble woman learned to hem and embroider their own underwear, handkerchiefs and bed linen. Many of Holbein's portraits show the details of this home industry which was considered a genteel activity for women. Marie seems to have passed the hours of her captivity in two ways: writing letters and embroidering panels of canvas. She had the help of Pierre Oudry an artist and professional embroiderer who drew the outlines of her designs, and these in turn were copied from engravings by Pierre Belon, Conrad Gessner and other contemporary artists. Some of the work was carried out at Chatsworth, others at Tutbury and the other places she was held at during her captivity.

There are about 120 panels of embroidery on display at Oxburgh Hall in Norfolk, some by Bess of Shrewsbury and others by Marie Stuart. Others are at the Victoria and Albert (V&A) Museum in London. An inventory taken at Chartley, after Marie's execution, lists several hundred worked pieces, many presumably embroideries.

It is intended to put the collection on permanent display at Tutbury Castle, the scene of so many events recorded in this book and one where Marie Stuart may have worked on some of the original embroidered panels. I believe there is a case to be made for considering Marie Stuart to have been a Staffordshire personality, through her long years of incarceration in this county, and one who might have graced the throne of England had historical events taken a slightly different turn.

Roger Joy, June 2004

The remains of the 12th century Chapel at Tutbury Castle.
Mary was lodged at Tutbury Castle for four separate periods during the 19 years that Elizabeth I kept her prisoner before eventually signing her execution warrant. *Courtesy of Dr Roger Joy.*

Mary Queen of Scots in Westminster Abbey   *Courtesy of Dr Roger Joy.*

Lesley Smith, the Curator of Tutbury Castle, as Mary Stuart.   *Courtesy of Dr Roger Joy.*

Chapter 7
Mary Queen of Scots

Mary Queen of Scots married her second husband Henry Stuart, Lord Darnley, on 29th July 1565. Unfortunately, the young couple did not live happily ever after. Mary soon found out that her new spouse simply was not good husband material and by the time their son James Stuart was born in June 1566, he had turned into an outright liability, neither faithful, companionable nor even a good political ally.

It seems that Mary may have been aware of and even involved in the plot that removed Darnley from the scene. At any rate, she happened to be sleeping elsewhere on the night that his house in Kirk o' Field was blown apart. Unfortunately for the plotters, Darnley somehow survived the explosion and had to be strangled as he was escaping from the ruins of the property. His half-naked corpse was found in the grounds and a broken neck belied any suggestion that his death was a tragic accident. He had without doubt been the victim of a clumsy assassination.

Elizabeth I showed a great deal of concern at the rumours of Mary's implication in Darnley's death. Mary did nothing to appease the English Queen's concerns when, within three months of being widowed, she married the very man who was suspected of murdering her husband - James Hepburn, Earl of Bothwell. This, her third union, turned out to be as short lived and disastrous for Mary's reputation as her second one. She lost the loyalty and support of her subjects and was forced to abdicate in favour of her baby son James and flee Scotland.

She was 25 years of age when on 15th May 1568 she clandestinely boarded a fishing boat and crossed the Solway Firth seeking friendly English soil. She assumed that sanctuary and assistance would be forthcoming from her fellow Queen and kinswoman, Elizabeth. As so often in Mary's life, she got it completely wrong. Queen Elizabeth had no intention of welcoming into her Court a woman with such a strong claim to the English throne, and the circumstances of Darnley's death gave her the excuse to keep Mary at arms length. But she did not allow the Scots Queen to return to Scotland or cross the Channel to France either. For the rest of her life, Mary remained Elizabeth's prisoner.

The two women never met although Mary bombarded Elizabeth with letters begging to be allowed at Court to 'put her side of the story'. Instead she was shunted from castle to castle as her relentless plans for escape, or plots to seize the English throne, were uncovered. When she first arrived in England she was taken to Carlisle Castle and there she was treated with every courtesy and consideration, but as time went on she was moved further and further away from the Scottish border, and her lodgings became increasingly less comfortable.

The worst of her prisons was Tutbury Castle. It was no longer a permanent residence by the mid 16th century and so when Mary first arrived there in the winter of 1569 it was inadequately furnished and in a state of dilapidation. Letters to supporters and friends complained bitterly of the cold and the lack of facilities. Her quarters there were so close to the privies that the stench was overpowering.

To help pass the idle hours of her captivity, Mary embroidered. She had learned needlecraft as a young girl in France at the knee of her mother in law, Queen Catherine de Medici. Later, in Scotland, she had worked at her embroideries as she sat at council meetings, endeavouring to learn the ways of the country she had come to rule. In those days of her young womanhood, when she was confident enough to cock a snook at the hand of Robert Dudley, the Earl of Leicester, it would never have occurred to her that she might come to rue her churlish behaviour. Did she ever regret her decision not to accept Queen Elizabeth's generous offer of marriage to her favourite courtier? As she designed and crafted the exotic creatures of her tapestries along with complicated monograms, anagrams and mottos, she certainly had the time to wallow in self pity and wonder how much more comfortable her life would have been if she had taken Robert Dudley as her Consort instead of Henry Stuart.

Likewise Robert himself. It was the only opportunity that Elizabeth ever gave him to marry with her blessing. When their passion for each other began to wane and Dudley took the fair young Douglas Howard Lady Sheffield into his bed, it was more than he dared do to admit to the Queen that he had married her and there is little but Lady Sheffield's word to say that he did, so their son, although he bore his father's name, was never accepted as legitimate.

As the years passed the Scots' Queen grew despondent, grey haired and arthritic in her cold, uncomfortable castle prisons while Elizabeth flirted outrageously with the next generation of courtiers and the occasional European potentate who still thought there might be a chance of becoming King of England.

Robert, by now reasonably certain that the Queen of England would never marry, not him nor anyone else, sought comfort in a low key marriage with Lettice Knollys, Countess of Essex. Elizabeth inevitably found out and in a fit of pique put him under house arrest. It was only a matter of days before she recalled him to her side, but she refused utterly ever to have poor Lettice at Court.

The year before this secret marriage, in the summer of 1577, Mary Queen of Scots met Robert Dudley. She was thirty five and he forty five. They had both travelled to Buxton to take the waters. Mary's health was poor and she suffered so dreadfully from arthritis that she had difficulty walking. Robert had lost his fine figure and was now overweight and florid, with a propensity to suffer from unspecified maladies.

Did Mary work at her embroidery while they chatted? What did they think of each other? Did they talk of what might have been - the security that marriage to the Earl of Leicester could have given her; the children, born to rule, that the Queen of Scots could have given him......?

THE DOWKER

The great crested grebe was called a Dowker in Tudor times. The original of this lovely design
is in remarkably good condition apart from the floral corner infills one of which
has completely disappeared. These corner infills occur on only two of the
replicated embroideries, the Dowker and the Poole Snyte.

The Dowker is not one of the slips appliqued to the Marian hanging at Oxburgh Hall, it also doesn't
carry Mary's monogram so perhaps cannot be attributed to her with certainty. Slips by the way are small
embroidered pieces applied to velvet or damask silk fabric and used mostly for utilitarian purposes like bed
hangings, skirts and cushions. This embroidery technique was very popular in Elizabethan and Jacobean
times. All of Mary's slips were worked exclusively in silk and on close examination one can distinguish
the variability in its thickness.

I found The Dowker a complicated piece for which to work out a stitch plan. Mary's finer gauge
proving to be a problem where she had shortened or extended stitches plus her overstitching for the crest
of the grebe; but I think this is a fair replication.   S.M.E.

THE BYRD OF AMERICA

A natural history book written in the mid 16th century by Swiss physician Conrad Gesner
and illustrated with woodcuts was the source of many of Mary's embroidered 'fantastick creatures'. The
embroiderer in her household, usually a man, would have drawn and
painted the design onto canvas ready for her to stitch.

The strange and new animals and birds of the New World, which had been known for less than 100 years
in Mary's time, would have been a wonderful inspiration for an embroidery designer. In his book, Gesner's
woodcut of the 'Byrd of America', a toucan, is depicted with a serrated edge to its beak; obviously Gesner
had never seen a toucan and was drawing from second or even third hand knowledge. It is probable that
descriptions of these unknown creatures from the newly discovered continent developed into something
akin to the children's game of Chinese Whispers and transmuted into all kinds of oddities.

The original cruciform piece, along with most of the other embroideries I have replicated, was
appliqued on to green velvet and hung over the chimney breast in the King's room at Oxburgh Hall, Norfolk,
probably in the 18th century. Others were assembled similarly and used as bed hangings. For over two
hundred years they were housed in conditions most unfavourable to their preservation; consequently, this
piece is in very poor condition, many areas of stitching having rotted away; the 'Byrd's' beak had
disappeared completely with not a vestige of silk left. After liaising with the V & A (owners of the hangings)
and discussions with Dr Joy, the decision was taken to work the beak in cream; I would have preferred
yellow but was outvoted.   S.M.E.

THE OCTAGON MONOGRAM

This artfully worked monogram (puzzles, devices and rebuses delighted the Tudor court)
is one of the pieces that can be attributed with certainty to Mary Queen of Scots
containing her personal cipher, an M superimposed with the Greek ϕ. On starting to work on this
embroidery I was struck by the odd use of colours. The motto band is worked in yellow with the lettering
in cream making it almost unreadable. The 'T' in the monogram worked in pale fawn on cream not, I
thought, the expected choice of a woman renowned in her youth for her impeccable taste. On
researching Mary and her embroideries I found a possible reason for some of her strange colour choices,
she was kept short of materials - especially during her incarcerations in the detested Tutbury Castle
under the supervision of the equally detested Paulet - and frequently sent letters, mainly to her French
relatives, begging for silks.

Utilising the various upright strokes several times and the 'V' in the centre of the 'M' the letters in
the monogram spell her name MARIE STUART.

Mary used cross stitch in all these embroideries. It is worked with the top stitch always laid the same
way. Mary's are invariably laid top left to bottom right, but on inspecting the piece with a magnifying glass,
I noticed some anomalies, a run of twenty or so stitches laid in the opposite direction. What could have
caused this aberration in Mary's otherwise meticulous stitching? My own fantasy theory is that maybe her
work had been interrupted by the arrival of a clandestine message outlining yet another wild scheme for
her escape. Had she returned to her embroidery heart aflutter and head whirling with expectation and,
unthinking, embroidered those few stitches? Pure speculation? Maybe......   S.M.E.

THE PHENIX

The Phenix is depicted in the heraldic manner, arising from the flames. This device was taken from the seal of Mary of Guise, Mary's mother as was the motto embroidered on Mary's cloth of estate (canopy over a chair) used during her captivity -
'En Ma Fin Gịt Ma Commencement' - in my end is my beginning.
The original embroidery is in reasonably good condition and is authenticated by Mary's monogram.

    Creating a stitch plan of the Phenix was very time consuming mainly because of its speckled breast - a high powered magnifying glass proved indispensable. Mary had an advantage over me when it came to overstitching as when she worked the crest on the bird's head and the lettering. Her 'canvas' was more like fine hessian from what I can see where stitches have rotted away and she worked her cross stitch over two threads thus giving her leeway to work finer if needed. I was working on modern 14 count canvas and needed to be quite creative to replicate her effects.

    I am sometimes puzzled by Mary's embroideries. I wonder mainly why symmetry in certain things is ignored. The wings of the Phenix, the 'wobbly' crown in the octagon monogram are obvious to the eye - why didn't she see the strangeness of them? She wasn't working in a hurry, unlike Bess, Countess of Shrewsbury, her embroidery companion of many confined years, who churned out embroidery by the yard in her haste to furnish her newly built opus magnum, Hardwick Hall.   S.M.E.

THE POOLE SNYTE

The Poole Snyte (a Tudor term for the great snipe) was yet another embroidery
in Mary's zoological collection, many of them embellished with Latin mottoes
which were seemingly innocuous but which often could be interpreted
as a barbed message intended for her tormentors.

The Snyte embroidery is one of two which have corner infills, depicted in this piece are snails and butterflies. To the Elizabethans, most things - flowers, animals, insects etc. carried hidden messages, abstract concepts such as love, freedom, jealousy. It is well known that the butterfly symbolised freedom; the snail is a little ambiguous - perhaps the crawling pace of time to a prisoner.   S.M.E.

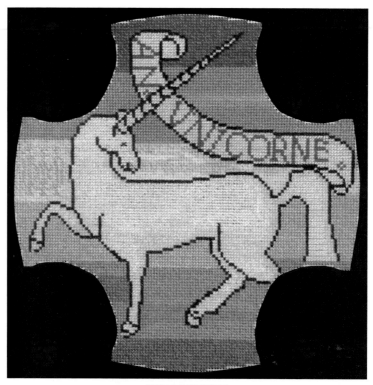

THE UNICORN

Yet another fabulous beast from Mary's zoo. At this period of discovery and exploration, people were still unsure as to whether this animal was fact or fiction.

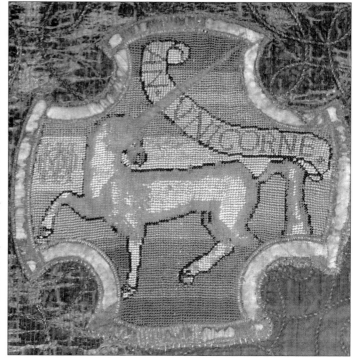

The original piece, on the right, was badly worn and rotted and the actual shading of the body of the unicorn was difficult to decipher, but the embroidery looks good restored to my interpretation.

The final piece to be worked will be 'The Dolphin'. Dr Joy kindly gave me carte blanche for the choice of the last embroidery and 'The Dolphin' seemed to me to be a perfect symbol for Mary's earlier, happier life. The Dolphin (or Dauphin in French), was the title held by the eldest son of the King of France. Francis, Mary's young husband held that title but their time as Dauphin and Dauphiness of France was tragically short, the sickly Francis dying within a year of their marriage. That she remembered and perhaps was even fond of him shows in her monogram used in her embroideries. Francis was her Omega - the last.   S.M.E.

HENRY VIII

One of the most recognisable of all English monarchs, Bluff King Hal was Mary's great uncle. She certainly exhibited quite a few of the Tudor family traits, wilful and stubborn - with an occasional lapse into heart ruling head, in her case disastrously.

Henry was my first large embroidery, taken from the famous Holbein portrait. The idea that I didn't want to work this piece in just tent stitch was formulating as I worked on the design. He was such a majestic and imposing character, he needed to stand out. Those words were the key - three dimensional - and my appliqué worked and 'jewel encrusted' style came into being.

Henry VIII and his six wives was my plan. After working Henry, Jane Seymour was next, then Anne Boleyn, but the series got no further I'm afraid because in mid-1994 my inspiration for the Staffordshire Millennium Embroideries struck and the Tudor saga was abandoned. S.M.E.

MARY QUEEN OF SCOTS ARRIVES AT TIXALL GATEHOUSE

THE 16TH CENTURY PANEL OF SYLVIA EVERITT'S 'STAFFORDSHIRE MILLENNIUM EMBROIDERIES'

In 1586 Mary was held prisoner in Tixall Hall while her apartments at Chartley Manor were searched for evidence of a plot against Queen Elizabeth. Incriminating documentation was discovered and Mary was executed on the strength of it.

The choice of centre point for the 16th century panel was a fortuitous coincidence - little did I know that in Millennium year I would begin a series of replicas of Mary Queen of Scot's embroideries. A small tribute to a tragic Queen who spent long periods of imprisonment within our county.   S.M.E.

The Staffordshire Millennium Embroideries are on permanent display at the Lichfield Heritage Centre, Market Square, Lichfield. Telephone 01543 256611 or www.lichfieldheritage.org.uk

Dianne's history book based on the Embroideries can also be obtained there or from the publishers.